Ola Nylander

Architecture of the Home

Translated by John Krause
and Deborah Fronko

WILEY-ACADEMY

Other Wiley Editorial Offices

John Wiley & Sons Inc., 111 River Street, Hoboken, NJ 07030, USA

Jossey-Bass, 989 Market Street, San Francisco, CA 94103-1741, USA

Wiley-VCH Verlag GmbH, Boschstr. 12, D-69469 Weinhelm, Germany

John Wiley & Sons Australia Ltd, 33 Park Road, Milton, Queensland 4064, Australia

John Wiley & Sons (Asia) Pte Ltd., 2 Clementi Loop #02-01, Jin Xing Distripark,
Singapore 129809

John Wiley & Sons Canada Ltd, 22 Worcester Road, Etobicoke, Ontario, Canada M9W 1L1

ISBN 0–470–84787–5

Designed and typeset in 10/14 Galliard by Florence Production Ltd, Stoodleigh, Devon EX16 9PN
Printed and bound in Great Britain by T.J. International Ltd, UK
This book is printed on acid-free paper responsibly manufactured from sustainable forestry in which
at least two trees are planted for each one used for paper production.

Contents

Preface

This book is based on my doctoral thesis, 'The individuality of the home' (October 1998). I conducted my research in the Theoretical and Applied Aesthetics unit of the Department of Building Design at the Chalmers University of Technology School of Architecture in Gothenburg, Sweden.

In revising the text for this edition, I have retained its scientific and academic organization, including problem descriptions, case studies and results. My alterations consist primarily in a redevelopment of the specifically research-oriented parts of the text. I have downplayed the orientation of my work within the field of research and the explanation of my methodology. I have also simplified the documentation of sources.

It has been inspiring to revise the text for publication by John Wiley. The revisions have largely entailed making references more international. The ideas put forward in the book derive from Swedish and Scandinavian conditions. However, as my purpose with the book is to describe a relationship to architecture and spatial attributes, the results are also generally applicable to the home and the idea of dwelling in a broader sense. Architecture's impact on the experience of dwelling is a factor that is similar for homes in many countries.

Ola Nylander
Gothenburg, Sweden
January 2002

Acknowledgements

Financial support from the Lars Erik Lundbergs Stipendiestiftelse and Helgo Zettervalls fond foundations has made this translation possible, and is gratefully acknowledged.

Photographs are by Sten Gromark, Inger Bergström, Ulf Nilsson, Charles Hörnstein, Göran Peyronsson, Marie Hedberg, Jappe Liljedahl and Sune Sundahl.

Many people have helped and supported me during the work. Foremost among them are my advisor, Associate Professor Sten Gromark, and the chairman of my review committee, Professor Armand Björkman, who together piloted my work to its destination. Marie Hedberg read and criticized the revised text.

Essential to my work were the many residents and architects who kindly submitted to my requests for interviews. The four housing corporations who own the apartments that were the subjects of my case studies, Bostadsbolaget (Gothenburg), AB Boråsbostäder (Borås), HSB (Karlskrona), and Ståhls Byggnads AB (Norrköping), provided me with architectural plans and other practical information that helped me prepare for the interviews.

Sources of illustrations

Unless otherwise stated, photographs have been taken by the author. All interviews were recorded on tape, and are in the author's archives along with the transcripts.

Case study Lindholmen was built by Västsvenska Bygge and Bostad AB for the municipal housing company Göteborgs stads Bostads AB.

Case study Stumholmen was built by JM Byggnads AB for HSB Karlskrona.

Case study Hestra was built by Fristad Bygg AB for the municipal housing company AB Bostäder, Borås

Case study Norrköping was built for and by Byggnads AB Henry Ståhl.

Chapter 1

Introduction

As a boy I spent many summers in my grandfather's old house in Dalsland County. It was technically antiquated, and we had to fetch water from a well some distance from the house. Cooking was done on a wood stove or a little kerosene burner, and at dusk each night we lit kerosene lamps. One of the few technical features of the house was the battery-powered transistor radio we sometimes listened to.

It was in many ways a wonderful house. It seemed carefully designed for all of the games my brother and I played during a few intense summer months. There was a front porch, a huge kitchen, and a room that was just there, between the entrance hall and the kitchen, without an apparent purpose. The whole family slept together in the great room, and the elegant parlour was off limits. The floors were wood, the walls panelled with beaded boards, and sunlight filtered through divided-light windows, warming the flagstones outside the

The summer house, photograph from our album. It seemed designed for all of the games my brother and I played during a few intense summer months.

kitchen door. Everything had a distinct sound and smell that strongly influenced my impression and my understanding of the old place.

In the city we lived in a spacious, newly constructed three-bedroom apartment. That was good, too, but in an entirely different way. Our apartment was well planned and modern, with two toilets and a telephone and television. My brother and I even had our own rooms.

He and I never discussed the differences between our home in the city and our summer home in the country, but I believe we both felt and understood them intuitively. Our grandfather's house played a central role in our image of summer, together with

swimming, boating and fishing. In the country we sometimes missed the city, too, but not for the apartment – what we longed for were our friends, our toys, the places we played and the pending start of the school term.

When I reflect now, some thirty years later, on various kinds of homes and ways of living, I realize that the difference between my two childhood homes has played an important role in my research. That influence was at first intuitive, and developed into an increasing consciousness of and insight into the importance of the poetic, sensory qualities of the home, and of its intimate connection with the existential. Certain buildings and places are perceived as more pregnant than others. My memories of our summer house are a good example, and I assume that many have had similar experiences.

During the course of my training at the School of Architecture at Chalmers, the curriculum for residential architecture was dominated by a technocratic approach typical of the day. The standards by which our student projects were judged were much the same as those defined by Swedish Building Standards and other official norms. By listening to lectures and diligently flipping through architectural journals, we students were inculcated into the profession's criteria for aesthetic evaluation. The architecture of place, like my grandfather's house in Dalsland, was never discussed by students nor the faculty.

In the years following my graduation I designed several residential projects in different contexts. I collaborated with others at various architecture firms in and around Gothenburg, including White Architects and K-konsult, and also worked independently, opening my own office in 1986. This period provided me with a chance to study the architecture of the home in greater depth. I began to appreciate the beauty of materials and detailing, and the pleasure of light-filled and easily comprehensible apartments.

During this time I had the opportunity to work on a large development of single-family detached homes in

Gothenburg. As architects our aim was to design buildings with squarish rooms, visual axes from one facade to the other, minimizing circulation space and maximizing ceiling height. We were quite in agreement on the value of these qualities. I found that, in discussions among architects, rarely was it necessary to describe them in detail – we took their value for granted.

However, there was a marked difference when we attempted to explain and defend our ideas in meetings with the other players involved in the construction process. The unanimous opinion of the architects was not enough to persuade builders, clients and developers. They wanted clear answers to questions such as: What's so good about a square room? What are the benefits of axial views through an apartment? What kinds of alternative, simpler materials are available?

None of us could offer any relevant arguments to address these questions. With no empirical evidence to support our claims we had a hard time convincing others that our particular proposal would give a better or more aesthetically pleasing result.

As is always the case with multi-family housing projects, we were working against a tight budget, and forced to modify our original visions in order to minimize costs. I sensed that many of the people involved in the project truly wanted to build beautiful, high-quality homes; in the end, nonetheless, most of the aesthetic qualities were eliminated for economic reasons. We were left with a functionally suitable but architecturally undistinguished housing development. In examining other new developments it became evident that other architects were struggling with the same problem.

I spent a lot of time thinking about these difficulties, frustrated at my inability to explain the importance of aesthetic qualities in residential architecture. As an architect among other industry consultants, I could defend without reservation only the functional requirements and standardized dimensions of the building code. Architects ought to have more to rely on than personal taste and our own individual aesthetic conceptions and design approaches.

The architectural qualities of the home

Inspired by the prospect of exploring the issues I had been brooding over in my practice, I returned to Chalmers University. It was natural for me to begin gathering information about the qualities and characteristics of residential architecture.

By the early 1970s, as an unprecedented campaign of housing development was drawing to a close, many realized the dilemma posed by focusing too heavily on the functional aspects of architecture. Researchers in other fields, such as ethnologists and sociologists, began to look for qualities and attributes that could not be quantified or captured in statistics. Residents were at the centre of their research.

One of the forerunners in this line of research was ethnologist Åke Daun, who in the early 1970s had described living conditions in newly constructed Swedish housing developments. Daun tried hard to fully comprehend what it was like to live in these areas. He had himself lived in one for a time, and through his many interviews and personal observations he succeeded in interpreting and describing something of the inherent complexity of home life.

Daun demonstrated that these new developments seldom provided sufficient opportunities for residents to establish a sense of territoriality. One of his research subjects was the Storvreten district outside Stockholm. Few of the residents he met were satisfied with their housing situation. The area suffered from a variety of problems including vandalism, litter, and conflicts between different social groups. One of the women he interviewed declared: 'I know what's wrong with Storvreten. There are just too many buildings in too small an area with too many people'.[1]

In her 1976 doctoral thesis, 'Idealbostad eller nödbostad' (Ideal home or emergency housing), architectural scholar Birgitta Andersson described two types of value placed on the home, two different ways of addressing residential issues – quality and quantity.

Andersson claimed that the proposals of politically motivated housing authorities in the years following the Second World War sacrificed quality in the interest of building as much quantity as possible. Good architecture was increasingly overshadowed by a growing interest in production techniques and economic issues. In the face of strong political and economic demands, architects failed to demonstrate the value of good design. Andersson cites several qualities that began to disappear during this era, including naturally lit stairwells, narrow buildings that allow daylight into apartments from two opposite facades, light-filled rooms, and a comprehensible scale and size.[2]

The effects of these developments, in which quantitative values were allowed to preclude qualitative, can be seen in our homes today. Many residents feel ill at ease in their apartments and find it difficult to make homes of them, despite their measurable, quantitative attributes.

The architecture of the home

What makes an apartment at once feel right, and why do some apartments quickly develop all the positive attributes and welcoming environment of a home? Author and social critic Ellen Key has offered a good description of what makes a home:

> There are magic rooms with amusement and delight in the air . . . There is an atmosphere that goes straight to the heart, a sense of mystery amidst the everyday, a kind of charge about the simplest things that animates them and gives reality a new dimension.[3]

The importance of creating meaning and the value of sensual perception have also been described by Christian Norberg-Schulz in his work on dwelling, in which he maintains that the task of the architect is twofold. Architects need to resolve a series of technical and functional issues, but the design of a building must also help its residents to appreciate and interpret the qualities of the site. Norberg-Schulz claims that architecture helps people to 'dwell' in the full sense of the word. Architecture is what makes living in a place more than merely the fulfilment of a practical need.

Applying Norberg-Schulz's analysis of dwelling to the multi-family housing project, two kinds of attributes can be distinguished: measurable functional attributes and non-measurable aesthetic attributes:

> While the satisfaction of practical requirements is based on measurable conditions and can be approached rationally, the realization of meanings is an artistic matter that relies on non-measurable quantities.[4]

The non-measurable architectural attributes of the home are an important part of the meaning and content of the lives of its residents. The architecture of the home must also be seen from an artistic perspective, however architecture is unique among the arts in that it has a substantial functional aspect. Norberg-Schultz holds that the home must be part of a 'poetic relationship to reality' and has an existential importance for residents as a bearer of meaning. The architectural attributes he describes are not pairs of opposites but rather a whole composed of two complementary parts. The goal for Norberg-Schultz is a balance or cohesion between practical and aesthetic qualities.

Elias Cornell, a professor of architectural history, makes similar observations, distinguishing between architecture's aesthetic and practical sides. Together the two provide a comprehensive picture of architecture's full significance. Cornell defines architecture as 'the aesthetic organization of practical reality'.[5]

The philosopher Gaston Bachelard suggests that a house is something that always plays a valuable role in the life of any individual. We are – willingly or not – cast out into the unknown, but only after a comforting period in 'the cradle of the home'. Space is both a foreign and irresistible medium. Bachelard discusses the qualities and attributes of the home that lie beyond the boundaries of objective, measurable space. He finds that these non-measurable attributes are difficult to capture in verbal descriptions. They are stored as memories within us, and we can reach their depths only with the aid of artistic expression, such as poetry. Bachelard describes the poetic qualities of the home as aspects that exist collaterally with its objective geometrical characteristics, using terms such as 'hidden magnitude', 'nearness', and 'depth': 'To give an object poetic space is to give it more space than it has objective'.[6]

Witold Rybczynski similarly describes the significance of the home in *Home – a Short History of an Idea*. A house both assembles and gives form to the feelings that infuse the idea 'home'. 'Domesticity has to do with family, intimacy, and a devotion to the home, as well as with a sense of the house as embodying – not only harbouring – these sentiments'.[7]

Measurable and non-measurable

I am convinced that the architecture of the home must be seen as the product of an integration of complementary measurable and non-measurable aspects. The measurable, practical, functional qualities of the home include all that we can physically delineate, measure and quantify. Its practical attributes have been carefully described in the housing research conducted in Sweden and other European countries since the 1930s. The resulting Building Standards regulations place demands on the practical functions of the home, including its furnishability, accessibility, mechanical equipment and systems such as heating and ventilation, and the planning of the exterior environment.

The non-measurable attributes of residential architecture are the qualitative, aesthetic and symbolic aspects that are important for our perception of the home.

The following quotation from my interview with the architect Bengt Lindroos (see Case study 4) provides a good description of the problem facing residential design:

> We need rules – it's a shame they're beginning to be undermined and to disappear. They were a guarantee that nothing could be really awful. But many of us are content to stop working as soon as we've satisfied the rules, when we're really only halfway there. And that's when the aesthetic qualities are just starting to take form.

The 'rules' to which Lindroos refers are the practical and measurable attributes described in the industry standards. Where, then, are we to look for 'aesthetic qualities'? My own experiences, as described earlier, suggest that many architects have an unclear vision of residential architecture beyond the functional and dimensional requirements of our housing standards.

Against the background of this introductory description, four questions may be distinguished as having guided my research:

- What are the non-measurable architectural attributes of the home?
- What forms do the non-measurable architectural attributes of the home take?
- What spatial variables and relationships influence our perception of the non-measurable attributes of residential architecture?
- What deeper significance do non-measurable architectural attributes have for residents?

Purpose

The purpose of my work is to answer these four questions – to identify, describe and analyse the non-measurable architectural attributes of the home – and thereby arrive at a more complete picture of residential architecture.

Identifying these attributes will show how they take form in the home and what significance they have for residents' perception of their homes.

The description is intended to conceptualize the non-measurable qualities of the home and thereby expand and clarify our understanding of the role they play in residential architecture.

One purpose of my analyses of the non-measurable architectural attributes of the home is to illustrate an element of the profession's tacit understanding of residential architecture.

Definitions

The concept of 'home' is central to my research. In this book I have chosen to limit my discussion of the home to rental units in multi-family apartment buildings: there is a comprehensive body of research on rental apartments, which provides a clear point of departure for my work, and limiting my research in this way also makes it easy to compare homes of equal size and technical sophistication. The design of rental apartments requires great skill from the architect: generalized requirements for anonymous users must be satisfied, often within a tight budget and within strict limitations.

Painting: 'Open doors', Wilhelm Hammershöi, 1908, private collection.

Chapter 2

Conducting architectural research

Architectural scholars who focus on housing research are fortunate in many respects. The real world offers an abundance of interesting answers – and questions. We need only to visit a variety of residential projects and discuss the architecture of the home with their residents and the architects who designed them.

Among architects, the traditional method of transferring knowledge of the profession is to build catalogues of exemplary prototypes – icons of architectural quality. Such a repertoire of prototypical apartments typically comprises projects that are published in professional journals and widely recognized in discussions of good residential environments. These buildings were designed by talented architects who understood and were able to convey the importance of the collective qualities of the home. Residents of these apartments have the opportunity to create in-depth relationships, meanings and quality of life. I have assumed that such homes will provide the conditions for uncovering and identifying non-measurable architectural attributes.

I have tried to utilize these prototypes in two ways: by studying the attributes of several of them and by composing my research as part of, or a more in-depth complement to a repertoire of prototypes. My aim has been to explain and describe the necessary conditions for those qualities identified and to critically evaluate the quality and content of various prototypical projects.

Qualitative research methods

The methodology used here favours a positive approach to research, and avoids the problematizing of conflict theories – a methodology that resonates with the traditions of the architectural profession.

A more common method of conducting housing research is to formulate and organize questions and then distribute questionnaires to residents. These generally use multiple-choice answers to evaluate residents' satisfaction with their apartments, neighbourhood, or other relevant aspects of such amenities. I consider the questionnaire-based study an inappropriate research method for uncovering the non-measurable attributes of the home. The brevity of questions and answers in questionnaire form makes it quite unlikely that one will discover anything unexpected, and diminishes one's sensitivity to the nuances of residents' and one's own perceptions. Questionnaire studies do suggest that non-measurable architectural attributes are profoundly meaningful to residents, which is extremely important. However, they give no indication of how or why they are so meaningful.

In many ways, the qualitative interview is the opposite of the questionnaire. Instead of statistically confirming a body of scientific facts through a large number of information sources, a few qualitative interviews are conducted and then interpreted by the researcher.

This has been the pattern for my work. I have tried to develop a research method that pays particular attention to the specifically architectural aspects of housing planning. The information base comprises both empirical sociological evidence derived from resident interviews, and analyses of relevant empirical architectural conditions and relationships.

My work has been inspired by the qualitative methods developed in the social sciences and humanities in which conceptualization and descriptions of qualitative values and attributes are important. The grounded theory method, developed by Barney Glaser and Anselm Strauss,[1] has been key to the development of my methodology.

My research can be divided into three parts: interviews with tenants who live in each case study project, interviews with the architects who designed these buildings, and finally a phase in which I, the researcher, organize, interpret and draw conclusions from the data.

Four case-study apartments

The architectural analyses carried out deal with the architecture of apartments on three levels: the materials and detailing, spatial figure and organization of the rooms. The analyses derive from conditions in Sweden and Scandinavia. However, as my purpose is to describe a relationship to architecture and spatial attributes, the results are also generally applicable to the home and the idea of dwelling in a broader sense. Architecture's impact on the experience of dwelling is a factor that is similar for homes in many countries.

I have chosen to work with objects that, though limited in number, are rich in content. The character and quality of observations are far more important than the number of observations in studying the kind of attributes in which I am primarily interested. In selecting case-study apartments, great importance has been placed on my personal perceptions of each, evaluating their depth of architectural meaning or feeling of well-being. My experience as an architect has also influenced my choices, since it allows me to intuitively evaluate the probability of finding relevant qualitative architectural attributes in potential objects. I have not attempted to describe the quantifiable aspects of non-measurable attributes should they appear. I have chosen a qualitative method because my objective is to describe certain qualities of the phenomena I might discover and identify. This qualitative and interpretive method has also proved well suited to another important part of my work – the analysis of residents' perceptions of their apartments.

Each of the four apartments I have chosen typifies the usual housing construction practices of its day. By contemporary standards they are all reasonably well planned in terms of area, mechanical equipment and cost. Each was created for a specific type of tenant and constructed on a good though not exclusive site.

The four apartments chosen for study are listed below:

1 *Case study Lindholmen* is a one-bedroom apartment built in 1992 in the Lindholmen district of Gothenburg. It covers 69m² (743 sq ft) and was designed by Armand Björkman of White arkitekter.
2 *Case study Stumholmen* is a two-bedroom apartment built in 1993 on the island of Stumholmen in Karlskrona. It covers 82m² (883 sq ft) and was designed by Kjell Forshed of Brunnberg & Forshed Arkitektkontor.
3 *Case study Hestra* includes several apartments in the Nielsen block of the Hestra development in the

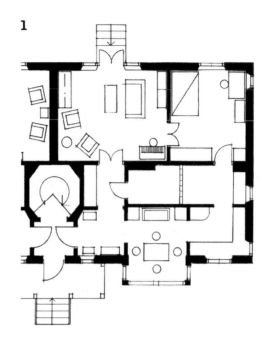

1

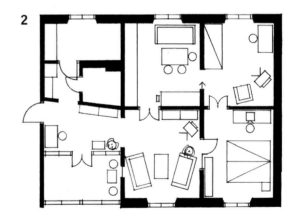

2

3

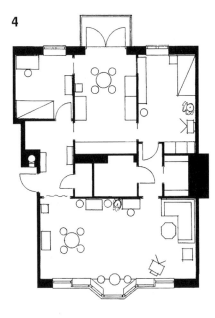

4

town of Borås that were built in 1992–3. The architect was Jens Thomas Arnfred of the Danish firm Vandkunstens Tegnestue.

4   *Case study Norrköping* is a two- or three-bedroom apartment in the Vattenkonsten block in Norrköping built in 1987. It has an area of 98 m^2 (1055 sq ft) and was designed by Bengt Lindroos.

The background for the above choices is more thoroughly presented later, in the description of each case study.

Scientific interpretation

My analyses of these case studies are attempts at a scientific interpretation of architectural perception. The background for this work is the group of architectural theory texts mentioned earlier. Four works that were particularly influential are: Christian Norberg-Schulz, *Mellom jord og himmel* (Between Heaven and Earth, in Norwegian only), 1978;[2] Gaston Bachelard, *The Poetics of Space*, 1964 (1958);[3] Dom Hans van der Laan,

Architectonic Space, 1983;[4] and Magnus William-Olsson, *Obegränsningens ljus* (The Boundlessness of Light, in Swedish only), 1997.[5]

The architecture of the four case studies is described with the help of various concepts and theoretical constructions, which are presented in Chapter 5, 'Fields of attributes: a more detailed characterization'. The attributes identified and the concepts described have acted as tools and potential perspectives in helping me process my impressions from apartment visits and interviews. I wish to emphasize that the identification and analysis of attributes often ran parallel to one another. I would also like to note that the relevance of various concepts and theories to a characterization of the perception of residential architecture was tested directly in the case studies.

The description of each case-study subject is integrated with quotations from my interviews with residents and architects. The point of these quotations is to give my presentation of each apartment greater fidelity with regard to how it is perceived by its inhabitants, and to enrich these presentations with the insights of the architects who designed the apartments.

Interviews

My interviews with residents and architects have been extremely important. Resident interviews provided important information in the search for significant architectural attributes. I was surprised by residents' understanding of the architectural attributes of the home, and their ability to communicate information about them, especially after the difficulty I personally have experienced in communicating about architecture with non-architects. As I put together the transcripts from these interviews for this book, I was particularly fascinated by several of their comments. One such comes from an interview with Karin, who lives in the Hestra development in Borås:

Interviewer: It sounds like a form of love at first sight.

Karin: Yes, it was – I thought the apartment was ... I don't know, it was everything about the place. Part of it was that it wasn't the traditional, rectangular kind of construction, partly that there was so much light, and then that it had natural materials everywhere. Our last place had plastic trim and vinyl flooring. And then just the architecture. The light and the location – you look right out into nature.

I realized later that Karin had touched on six important areas, or fields of attributes: materials, daylight, spatial figure, enclosure, and organization of spaces.

My work with the case studies began in 1995 and concluded in 1997. To some extent, practical conditions influenced the structure of each case study. An important prerequisite for such studies was the willing participation of the architects, residents and landlords.

The interviews with residents were between one and two hours long and concluded with a tour through each apartment, photographic documentation, and an inventory of furnishings. The interviews with architects were conducted in their offices. All interviews were tape-recorded, and the transcription of each was sent to the appropriate resident or architect for their comments.

Stumholmen. Window in living room, towards the loggia. Photo: Göran Peyronson.

Chapter 3

Identifying fields of attributes

My survey of the historical development of Swedish housing suggested that qualitative aspects are now on the verge of eclipsing the quantitative approach that has dominated housing construction since the 1960s. This puts the focus on questions such as, What are the non-measurable architectural attributes of the home?, and What is it about apartments that makes people enjoy living in them and allows them to create a sense of home?

My research has led me to identify seven groups of attributes that I consider significant for our perception of the home. I have chosen to call these groups 'fields of attributes'. A field of attributes is that distinguishable complex of details, attributes and characteristics I have tried to identify and describe in the case studies.

These fields of attributes are well known and are much represented in architectural history. I have evaluated their relevance for describing our perceptions of residential architecture. Fields of attributes have aided in my observations and analyses of the home. My awareness and description of the seven fields have developed gradually during the course of my research. Identifying attributes and analysing apartments often proceeded as parallel aspects of a single process. Each case study has contributed to the discovery and identification of important fields of architectural attributes. At the same time, working with the case studies has also allowed me to evaluate the relevance of various concepts and theories to our perception of the architecture of the home.

The fields of attributes I have identified are:

- Materials and detailing
- Axiality
- Enclosure
- Movement
- Spatial figure
- Daylight
- Organization of spaces

Materials and detailing

The choice of materials and design of the details are key elements in our perception of the home. The concepts of appropriation, care and authenticity are the cornerstones of our perception of materials and detailing. The word appropriation, derived from the French, means to make something one's own. The concept has been developed in many sociological housing studies by such scholars as Henri Lefebvre.[1] Appropriation is the process by which a person incorporates his home into his life, and familiarity with the materials of the home influences his relationship to it. Architectural scholar Eva Hurtig uses appropriation to describe the process by which a person makes a house into a home. Security, identity and familiarity are some of the important concepts Hurtig uses to illuminate the importance of the home.[2]

If high-quality materials and detailing can be interpreted by residents as signs of consideration for their well being, then they can initiate the process of appropriation. The perception of authenticity in materials depends on several important factors: one must have some understanding of how the material is produced, how it is worked, and a sense of time and history in how it is used.

The development of the home, from the late nineteenth century to the present day, is evidence of important changes in materials and detailing. The traditional middle-class home was richly worked, with heavily moulded trim, ceiling rosettes, patterned parquet floors and panelled wood doors. The transition to Functionalism brought with it the simplification of architectural details with the intention of creating a more rational home environment. During the 1940s and 1950s, profiled mouldings were smoothed out, and window and door trims were simplified.

Until the 1950s, housing construction was characterized by traditional craftsmanship. The acceleration of construction during the 1960s meant more prefabrication and industrialization in the building industry. During the early Functionalist era, details had been simplified for aesthetic reasons, and the changes only increased their precision and significance. But in the 1960s, the continual simplification of details degenerated in many respects into flimsiness. This trend continued during the 1970s and 1980s as more and more elements of the home were prefabricated for quick installation on site with less and less labour. The traces of craftsmanship became increasingly rare in new construction.

Traditional building materials such as stone, wood, steel, brick and plaster were joined by many new materials during the twentieth century. A variety of plastics, sheet materials and insulation products replaced and complemented the stock of traditional materials, with some of these new products imitating traditional materials, for example wood-grained vinyl flooring and plastic trim.

Appropriation and care

The creation of space is the construction of meaning. In the relationship between resident, site and home, appropriation is the process – the human action – by which the social consequences of architecture are generated. Appropriation is how residents incorporate space and architecture into the patterns and projects of their lives.

> Good architecture is that which is from the user's point of view genuine and authentic . . . The process of appropriation can be seen as a fundamental part of this authenticity, of this genuineness in the form and content of architecture. Appropriation is the course of events by which man invests buildings and urban spaces with meanings and connotations that are both personal and widely shared.[3]

Materials and detailing can begin the process of appropriation by signalling care for the residents. Their perception of care is intimately connected with how they identify with their homes. Signs of care can heighten a resident's sense of self and are interpreted as indications that the resident is important to someone. Architecture can thus fulfil our need for personal dignity if it is interpreted as confirming the resident's value in society.

We shape and are shaped by our surroundings. Details that bear witness to care and consideration are perceived as positive. Certain materials can be perceived as pregnant with associations and feelings. In this light, the mutability of a material is significant: its ability to be reworked or marked with the traces of previous events is important to our perception.

When a resident appropriates his or her home, he or she occupies its rooms and establishes a sense of territory inside and out. The process leads to identification,

Materials and detailing can begin the process of appropriation. Detail from single family home in Onsala.

an intimate relationship between the resident and the home.

Architectural scholar Bobo Hjort describes identification as 'man's sense of where he is at home'.[4] The authenticity of materials can demonstrate a comprehensible context, a recognizable experience or historic affinity.

The materials of the home contain historical and symbolic signs that we can relate to or interpret; whether this is easy or difficult depends on the nature of the materials. We seem to appreciate materials that are not overly smoothed. An example is the relationship between the perception of care, signs of craftsmanship and richness of architectural detailing:

People have been at work here, craftsmen have been here; they've invested love and a lot of consideration, and I think people like that – that it's not so barren, so generalized, because it expresses something . . . A smooth surface is dead – that's most people's spontaneous reaction.[5]

Care for residents can be conveyed either through well thought-out and well executed details or through the symbolic value inherent in certain details and materials. An environment with poorly executed, sloppy details, or one that is devoid of details has the opposite effect: it conveys a negative message – that those responsible for the design were not particularly interested in their job.

Authenticity is important to our perception of the care embodied in materials and details. The Greek

'People have been at work here, craftsmen have been here; they've invested love and a lot of consideration, and I think people like that – that it's not so barren, so generalized, because it expresses something'. Andersson, Torbjörn: 'Människan och miljön' (People and the environment, in Swedish only), p 53, in the journal *Miljonprogrammet* (The Million Programme, a common designation for the building boom of the 1960s), ed. Mats Theselius, Stockholm, 1993. Photo: Sten Gromark.

The space of the forest. Timeless space. Space for freedom. A space that is opposite to the space of the city. A part of our common consciousness and memory.

origins of the word suggest trustworthiness. We can feel close to a material only if we understand it. Around the beginning of the twentieth century, architects searched explicitly for a more genuine materiality in their work. A genuine material was considered one that did not hide its nature or imitate other materials.

Architectural scholar Professor Sven Hesselgren points out that certain materials are more difficult to work than others. Plastics, for example,

show the same architectural difficulty, i.e. the difficulty of giving an object created in this material a good expression of the material. . . . From the beginning, plastic objects have been imitations of other forms.[6]

According to Hesselgren, due to culture we recognize certain materials more readily than others. Through past experience we can get a sense of a material's substance or physicality.

Our understanding of the symbolic value of materials and details is influenced by our collective memory – our common history and cultural background.

One can sense a relationship to nature in genuine building materials. Each plank of an old pine floor seems to speak of its origins, from the felling of a tree in the woods to its treatment in a sawmill. This is the kind of easily comprehensible relationship that makes something seem genuine.

The careful installation of the dressed planks in the rooms of an old house also reveals traces of a previous generation's work. Wooden planks have been joined together to make a floor with the help of simple hand tools. The planks lie side by side, the width of each given by the thickness of the tree trunk. Each plank is marked with the footsteps of former generations. The softer early wood between annual rings has been worn down and scoured out with soap and water over the years, leaving the harder late wood raised like a relief carved by history.

We can read and interpret all of this. The origin, production and use of materials are part of our common consciousness and memory.

Even where there is great difference between a new wood floor and the broad pine planks of the past, they share the ability to convey the perceptual trinity of origin, production and use. The symbolic value of the old plank floor has been transferred to today's polished wood floor. Our understanding of this trinity is one of the main reasons behind the difference in our ability to feel close to wood as opposed to plastics. Few of us have any understanding of how vinyl flooring is made or worked. Unlike wooden floors, vinyl is irreparable. Everyday wear on a vinyl floor eventually causes it to fall apart. When the producers of vinyl flooring realized the positive associations we have with wood, they began to make patterns that imitate wood floors. Plastic laminate flooring even contains a photographic image of real wood imprinted within the plastic.

In summary, the concepts of appropriation, care and authenticity are important cornerstones for our perception of the materials and detailing of the home. If materials and details can be interpreted as signs of care for residents, then they can initiate the process of appropriation. Our perception of authenticity in a material depends on our awareness of its origins, understanding of its production and the sense of time and history conveyed by its use in the home.

Facade, Äskhults by (an old preserved village dating from the eighteenth century, about 30 km (19 miles) south of Gothenburg). Each individual plank seems to speak of its origins.

Axiality

Directional axes provide an example of the ability of residential architecture to express a strong feeling of presence. The perception of axiality in the home begins when we find ourselves at the starting point of an axis. The visual impression of an axis creates anticipation that we can confirm by moving along its direction. Axiality lends a direct physical relationship to our perception of the architecture of the home.

Circulation and directional axes can connect the rooms of a home with one another. This makes it possible to observe the light and atmosphere of one or more rooms from an adjoining room, making the apartment easy to survey.

Directional axes can visually emphasize and highlight important aspects of the home. Axiality is part of, and contributes to, residents' appropriation of their apartments. It is also important to the integration of interior and exterior space when directional axes lead to important points of contact between inside and out.

Axiality has long played a prominent role in the spatial organization of architecture. Symmetrical axes were important elements in the ceremonial complexes of the ancient Egyptians. Axiality and symmetry were also significant characteristics of urban planning at the time of the Roman Empire, where a common central theme was the axis that led to a ceremonial image. After the discovery of the cross vault, Roman interiors too were informed by a system of crossing axes. The cross

Cross vault, reconstruction of Maxentius Basilica.

vault made it possible to create larger spaces than previously and to give a room two equally important perpendicular axes. Transverse axes gave rhythm to the dominant longitudinal axis, and floor plans were often developed around a single or repeated crossing of axes.

The axis was also a common theme during the Renaissance period. It was Bramante who reintroduced axial planning in the late sixteenth century, by organizing buildings around directional axes and choreographing the architectural experience as a movement through axial chains of contiguous rooms. This axial order could also be used to integrate a building with existing axes in its surroundings. During the Rococo period, axes through chains of rooms were moved from the centreline of the spaces towards the outside walls to allow them to work together with the influx of daylight.

From the seventeenth century onwards, throughout the Western world axiality was one of the most

Axial order: Villa Rotonda – entry, Andrea Palladio, begun in 1567.

Choreographed movement through axial chains of contiguous rooms. Ottobeuren, early eighteenth century. Photo: Inger Bergström

prominent features of the classically inspired middle-class home. Rooms for formal entertaining – hall, anteroom, parlour, and dining room – were often aligned and interconnected. Passageways, service corridors and the less important rooms facing the courtyard might also be arranged axially.

The ideas of the Arts and Crafts Movement changed the use of axiality in the home. Suites of walk-through rooms were replaced by radial groupings of rooms entered from a central hall. Axiality appears only occasionally in the Functionalist apartments built from the 1930s onwards. An important element of these space-saving and functionally segregated apartments is the hall that provides access to each of the other rooms. There is no integration among bedrooms, kitchen and living room. This layout pattern became even more dominant during the 1960s and 1970s.

Axial composition

The Penguin Dictionary of Architecture defines axiality as follows: 'Of a building planned longitudinally or along an axis' (1980 edition, p. 26).

In Harris, *Dictionary of Architecture and Construction*, 2nd edition, axis has the following meaning: 'A straight line indicating the centre of symmetry of a solid or plane figure'.

Axial composition in the home can have both physical and symbolic aspects. Its physical aspects are how a directional axis is designed; its symbolic significance is the effect of axiality on a resident's perception of his home.

Professor Emeritus Jan Wallinder points out the ordering role of the orthogonal plan's inherent axiality: 'The primary axes of the home – parallel and perpendicular to the facade – are the basic starting points for the organization of the plan'.[7] He sees axiality as the result of the influx of daylight and interpenetrating sight lines, and calls this one of the tools available to residential architects for creating an eventful home.

An architectural axis is a line that connects two interesting points and to which spaces relate. This characterization is more far-reaching than the symmetrical relationship described in *The Penguin Dictionary of Architecture* definition. An axis must spring from something meaningful and indicate a direction from that point. Where two axes meet, the architectural event is intensified.

Christian Norberg-Schulz describes the axial complex of spaces as part of an active relationship between nature and the built environment. In many buildings of the late Renaissance there is an interplay between interior and exterior spaces and circulation patterns along axial lines. Norberg-Schulz points out that this creates a relationship between the building and its surroundings in the architecture of this period. Architecture is thereby an active element in the dialogue between the individual and the world around him or her. Space is experienced and 'conquered' through activity, by

Ny Carlsberg Glyptotek, Architect: Hack Kampmann 1901–06. Copenhagen. Axiality through a chain of symmetrically interpenetrated uniform rooms.

moving along a directional axis – a means of symbolically taking possession of the place.[8]

To summarize, axiality can visually emphasize important elements of the home. It can dramatize circulation patterns and daylighting conditions. Axiality can also be used to organize the rooms of an apartment, whether as symmetrically interpenetrated sequences of

Gunnebo Manor House, axial composition, building–site. Photo: Boris Schönbeck.

spaces or as sight lines that visually connect important elements. Our perception of axiality is tied to movement, daylighting and the organization of spaces.

Enclosure

Bachelard's description of the relationship between a house and a wintry landscape gives us an understanding of how our perception differs between open and enclosed space in the home. He asks the reader, 'Isn't it so that a nice house makes winter more poetic, and doesn't winter give poetry to the house?'. What is essential is the contrast in the relationship between the characteristics. Bachelard continues, '. . . and we feel the warmth [inside the house] precisely because it's cold outside'.[9]

The impression of openness or enclosure is of great importance to our perception of residential architecture. Openings in outside walls establish the character of the relationship between inner private space and the public space outside. Each opening demonstrates the implications of the boundary between the two. The divided-light window set within thick masonry walls creates an atmosphere of security inside in relation to the unknown space beyond. Glazing bars modulate the effect of a hole in the wall, and a deep embrasure accentuates the enclosing wall's sheltering capacity. The confinement of the little interior room is clarified and contrasted by its juxtaposition with the boundless exterior. The home thus becomes a solid point of security that makes it possible for the individual to appropriate and identify with even the world outside. As Juhani Pallasmaa so aptly describes this experience, 'The experience of home is never stronger than when seeing the windows of one's house lit in the dark winter landscape'.[10]

The perception of open and closed has different values for an individual over time. For many people, the closed space symbolizes security and safety – it is something positive. At the same time, open space can symbolize freedom and expansion – a symbol of opportunity.

If, for example, we are in a phase of boredom with being closed in at work, in life, by our parents or whatever, then we want to get out – to expand – and then I believe that we read the sea or openness as universal symbols of opportunity. . . . This even influences our view of a housing development: is it closed, and how do I relate to it? Closed spaces can be positive for most of us, because as a rule they appeal to our need for security and coziness, just as the sky and a distant view appeal to our need for openness.[11]

Historical changes

There is a clear and important line of division between Classical and Modernist architecture in terms of spatial enclosure versus openness. Modernist space strives for openness, a symbiosis between interior and exterior space, while the Classical room has a fixed relationship – a clear delineation – between inside and out.

Once the box has been dismembered, the planes no longer form closed volumes, containers of finite

Glazing bars modulate the effect of a hole in the wall and accentuate the enclosing wall's sheltering capacity.

Free-floating space in the home, Villa Savoye, Poissy, Le Corbusier, 1928–31. Photo: Sten Gromark.

spaces. . . . The static quality of classicism is replaced by a dynamic vision.[12]

In the historical development of the home, the distinctly enclosed room has dominated. In the Classical middle-class home, rooms are clearly enclosed. Wall openings are relatively few and small, and the walls themselves radiate weight and mass. In the Arts and Crafts inspired apartments of the early twentieth century there is a more liberal connection between the rooms. Larger windows with a low wall illustrate a new desire for contact and integration between interior and exterior space.

The free plan and the introduction of free-floating open space into the home emerged during the early decades of the twentieth century. Many of Frank Lloyd Wright's residential plans are characterized by spatial continuity between the various interior rooms. Ludwig Mies van der Rohe's pavilion for the Barcelona Exhibition of 1929 united this interior openness with an openness between inside and out.

Diffuse space was a sign of the times. Utility became an essential attribute for this new space. The goal then was to open the previously enclosed rooms of the home to sunlight and vegetation, but above all to the world outside. A new space was to replace the traditional space of the Western world, typified by Gothic and Renaissance room forms.

At the Siedlung Weisenhof Exhibition in Stuttgart in 1927, apartment interiors were shown with large openings, ribbon windows and spatially integrated rooms. The new steel-and-concrete construction technology made broad openings and non-load-bearing facades possible. But in practice the traditional enclosed room was never really questioned in postwar residential architecture. Instead, the apartments of the 1940s and 1950s were characterized by enclosed rooms of typical sizes, radially arranged about a neutral circulation hub. However, the spatial openness sought by Modernists did make an impact on urban planning. Open urban spaces dominated city planning from 1930 until the 1970s.

In many residential projects in Europe, the search continued for a deeper integration of open and closed

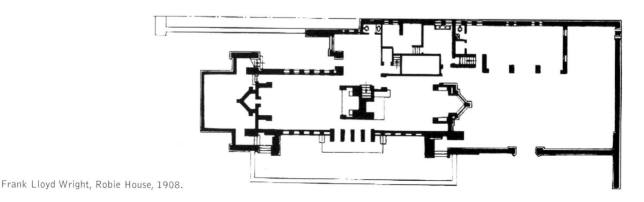

Frank Lloyd Wright, Robie House, 1908.

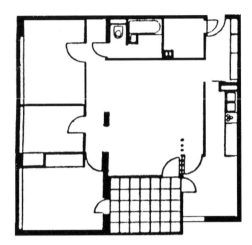

Interbau, Berlin, 1957.
Aalto's show apartment.

space in the home. Boundless openness was complemented by sequences of rooms in which a gradual transition from closed to open was sought.

Many apartments presented at the Interbau housing exposition in Berlin in 1957 exemplified the Modernist ambition of dissolving spatial boundaries. The architects of the time were working with unconstrained space and with diffuse and ambiguous boundaries. The various spaces in these exhibition apartments were delineated and integrated by layers of glass and glass doors. Norwegian architectural theorist Odd Brochman maintains that this openness is associated with the individual's need for recognition. In an open room we can be seen and thereby judged by the society outside, which would not be possible in an enclosed room.[13]

Open and closed space

In an open space, our attention is directed outward, beyond the room's borders. In addition to providing adequate daylight, a window can open a room by 'drawing our attention from the room to the view'. The same can be said of door openings. The rooms of the Modernist open plan are integrated with, and their focus directed towards, one another; in a closed room our attention is directed instead towards the walls of the room and the objects within it.

The clarity of space is altered by *continuity*, *enclosure* and *similarity*. We have the ability to interpret isolated parts as a whole. Therefore, it is easier for us to interpret a figure if it is enclosed by a contour.

Built architectural space must be seen in relation to the two archetypal existential spaces: the space of nature, the vast space between the earth's surface and the vault of the heavens, and the space of experience, the sphere of integrity that surrounds every person. We build architectural space by adding vertical walls to the horizontal surface of the space of nature.

We build these walls with material taken from the infinite mass of the earth. In the architectural space between these walls, a small part of the space of nature is conquered. A room thus delineated is transformed into a space of experience when we fill it with our experiences.

Architectural space is enclosed by mass. It is made visible by the form of the surrounding walls – by the form of the enclosing mass. Each room derives its intensity from the proximity, size and mass of these walls.

Openings in the walls make us aware of the space within and give us access to it. When we pass through these openings, we register the thickness – and therefore the mass – of the enclosing walls. In the case of a large opening, the wall is less important, functioning more as a frame around the opening. A small opening

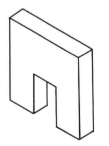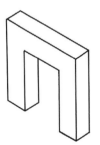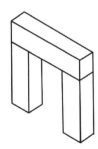

Development from an opening in the wall (figure to the left), towards a frame around the opening (figure to the right). Illustration from: *Architectonic Space*, Dom Hans van der Laan, Leiden, Brill, 1983.

Window in the lighthouse-keeper's residence, Nidingen's lighthouse station.

allows the form of the wall to be visible and clarifies its role as an enclosing mass. The size of openings in proportion to wall surface is a decisive factor in our perception of a space as open or closed. The character of that perception falls somewhere along a spectrum from confinement to a point where the enclosing attribute of the walls ceases to exist.

Architectural space is an invisible, imaginary room distinguishable from the visible concrete room. We can visualize the imaginary room through the proximity of our bodies to the surrounding walls. These walls have an architectural density that depends on their colour, wealth of detail and degree of affinity with other components.

The only entirely concrete space is that which is completely enclosed. We associate the openings or holes in an enclosed space with surrounding walls and close them with imaginary lines and surfaces. We use our imagination to perceive an enclosed space, the original, entirely enclosed space.

A space is an invisible volume of air . . . The visible makes up the form of a work. The invisible makes up its value . . . A space is a definite place in existence and as an idea it presents itself as an imaginary form . . . It is comprehensible as quality, as a conception, an illusion.[14]

Corners are important space-defining elements. Having the option of retreating to be left in peace in our corner gives us a sense of security. This creates an imaginary space around ourselves, the memory of which we carry within us. Bachelard describes the composition of architectural space as follows: 'Every corner of a house, every angle in a room, every inch of each room in which we usually hide or withdraw into ourselves is a symbol . . . That is the origin of a room or a house'.[15]

The home is in the same sense our protective corner of the world. Bachelard asserts that all inhabited space bears traces of the essential in our concept of home. A building is one of the strongest forces for fusing together our thoughts, memories and dreams.

Essential to a room's shape is the arrangement of its boundaries to neighbouring rooms. Bill Hillier and Julienne Hansson describe in *The Social Logic of Space* how this influences our way of identifying the home's spaces:

A building is therefore at least a domain of knowledge, in the sense that it is a certain spatial ordering of categories and a domain of control, in the sense that it is a certain ordering of boundaries . . .

Every building, even a single cell, identifies at least one inhabitant, in the sense of a person with special access to and control of the category of space created by boundary.[16]

Christian Norberg-Schulz describes the integration of interior and exterior space as an important part of how values are conveyed and meaning is accumulated:

Urban spaces tell of the possibilities of a place, but building interiors show what people have made of them . . . A building is a 'gift' because it makes our existence meaningful. Identification with the interior opens the world for us . . . To dwell in a landscape means to stake out an area, a place . . . We then create an 'inside' amidst the surrounding 'outside' . . . In this way we gain a foothold, and in this way identification becomes possible.[17]

We see the interior space of a house, the home, as our own little world, a place of refuge from the natural world outside. The design of the transition between inside and outside is critical to the clarification of the relationship between interior and exterior space. Sublime spatial densities establish an integration of building and site.

In summary, the enclosure of a room depends not only on the size of openings in its surrounding walls, but also on the clarity of its design. This clarity depends on, among other things, the readability of the space. Contours, corners and uninterrupted wall surfaces are important factors in the readability of a space. The boundary between open and closed in architectural space cannot be mathematically determined; what is important is the relationship between the two. Open and closed spaces have been valued differently over the course of history.

Movement

Creating a variety of possible movements and circulation patterns through the apartment increases the wealth of experiences we have at home. Like axiality, movement gives us a physical, corporeal relationship to the architecture of the home through the kind of movements described within axiality and through the rhythm of those movements. The tempo of our movement varies depending upon the size of the room: small rooms can be quickly read as we pass through them, while a larger room requires more time to survey. We subconsciously slow down to acquire information necessary to orient ourselves. This establishes a physical relationship between the human body and the size, shape and lighting conditions of a room, and to time. Pausing in the larger rooms gives our movement through an apartment a certain rhythm based on the form of its rooms. The rhythm of our movements is significant for our subconscious perception of the architecture of the home.

Magnus William-Olsson, the Swedish poet and literary critic, describes the active participation of the human body in the perception of art and the ability of poetry to move us. He claims that there is a connection between the act of reading and our perception of the text. We do not totally experience a poem until we read it aloud, thereby involving the body. Taking action is an important part of what William-Olsson describes as the ability of an encounter with art to touch the intuition and the unconscious. Poetry read aloud can convey a sense of reality and establish contact with the present moment.

Movement is defined in dictionaries as a physical concept. Architectural movement, however, is not bound by the laws of physics alone, but is also influenced by symbolism and personal experience.

Our understanding of space and its relationship to movement has evolved during the course of history. In the Western world, the concept of space is founded on the rooms of the ancients. The ancient room developed during the Roman Empire into a static space that symbolized imperial power. The semi-spherical space of the Pantheon is an example. Static Roman space became more dynamic during the Middle Ages. In the great Romanesque cathedrals, rhythm and movement were important elements in pilgrims' ceremonial procession past holy relics and images of saints.

During the Renaissance, the design of space focused on the individual, and secular building assumed an increasingly prominent role in the development of architecture. The ideal urban space of the Renaissance

The Pantheon, illustration by G. B. Piranesi.

of space. Fredrik Wulz summarizes this as follows: 'Architectural space always expresses time as well. One might say that architecture materializes time ... through the axial and plastic form of the space'.[18]

Movement is a precondition for experiencing architecture as a whole. Architecture invites movement, through space. Expectantly, we step forward and take possession of the architecture, of the building. We anticipate a continuation.

Architectural scholar Inger Bergström describes how architecture can influence our movement through space choreographically. Forms can attract or repel us, and the active, physical relationship of our movements to architecture is a strong influence on our perception. Bergström asserts that there was a time when we were

differed greatly from the enclosed places of the Middle Ages. Medieval streets were often bent, which interfered with lines of sight and extended views. Renaissance rooms were easy to survey, that is they could be taken in at a glance, and the urban spaces of the era were calculated and balanced, reposing and peaceful. They became more dynamic in the Baroque period, as the enclosing wall surfaces and ceilings were animated by a powerful plasticity. The distinguishing pathos of the Baroque era was its movement, a rhythmic movement. Baroque urban spaces were composed of intentionally unbalanced elements: places charged with tension.

Attempts were made in the first decades of the twentieth century to expand the concept of space by adding a fourth dimension – time. Le Corbusier's Villa Savoye is an example of this new vision of space-time in which the experience of architecture is planned as an orchestrated movement through the free plan of a building. Awareness of the relationship between time and architecture has become an important part of our concept

The Pantheon. Photo: Marie Hedberg.

much more aware of how various architectural forms affected our movement through space; however, that knowledge has for several reasons been lost.[19]

Sven Hesselgren describes two types of space – dynamic and static. Dynamic space can induce an observer to move through it. The observer strives to verify something by approaching the object. He or she examines it through movement. According to Hesselgren, we are encouraged to undertake such examinations by spaces that cannot be immediately surveyed or clearly read. The depth of a space can also provoke an observer to move along its axis.[20]

In the paintings of Vilhelm Hammershöi, a common motif is the movement through one room into another room beyond. Many of his works are organized around two well-lit rooms separated by a dim intermediary space. The figure of a woman, her back to the viewer, seems to be entering the room behind an open white door. The woman is turned towards, and in some cases seems to be moving towards, the light that emanates from the far side of the darkness. The white door appears to be a kind of symbolic boundary that must be breached before the dark intermediate space can be entered and traversed. Hammershöi's use of boundaries gives his paintings a sense of rhythmic movement by both distinguishing and demonstrating the contrasting character of different rooms.

Room function and movement

Our past experience of various room functions in-fluences our perception of space and our propensity for being induced to movement. Through our experi-ence – our personal history of prototypes – we associate street spaces with movement. The street space is a conduit through which traffic is led to public places. The street and the public square are the city's two fundamental spatial themes, one directional and one at rest. The conducting effect of the street can be strengthened or weakened by the plastic forms of the facades that enclose it. Smooth or strongly horizontal walls seem to increase the speed and ease of movement

Through our experience – our personal history of prototypes – we associate street spaces with movement. The street space is a conduit through which traffic is led to public places. Street scene from Vimmerby, Sweden.

through the street space. If the surrounding walls are heavily sculpted, they capture our attention and thus slow our movement along the street. Plasticity com-petes for our attention with the directional attraction of the goal at the end of the street axis.

This axiality can be either strengthened or weakened by the form of the street space. A visual landmark at the end of the street draws our attention from the surrounding walls to the landmark. The line of the eaves along the street can work as optical guidelines that enhance the dignity of the landmark. Gustav Strengell compares city streets and squares with natural phenomena: 'The movement of the street opens into the public square, where it comes to rest, in the same way a river flows into the sea'.[21]

If we translate this information about movement through urban spaces to rooms of the home, we find that rooms of various functions have historically been given specific spatial expression and spatial form. For example, the function of the hall as a circulation hub between the different parts of an apartment, and the living room's role as a gathering point, are important to our perception of movement and circulation within the home. Our conception of the general character of a space can be powerfully affected by accentuating or diminishing the impression of movement through the space.

Bill Hillier and Julienne Hansson describe the organization of space in traditional English housing and the potential that is created when rooms are connected to each other circularly. Freedom of movement through the home is created by giving each room two openings. The authors call this potential for movement, 'ringiness'.[22]

There is also common agreement about the tendency of certain architectural elements to stimulate movement. An example is the stairway, which can encourage various kinds of movement: though every stair in fact runs in two directions, we associate a cellar stair with a downward movement and an attic stair with an upward movement.

In summary, movement through the space of the home is critical to our experience of architecture. The design of space can invite movement. Movement comprises rhythm and direction and is directly connected to how we are subconsciously influenced by the form and organization of rooms.

Spatial figure

Spatial figure refers to the size and shape of a room in plan and section. The term spatial figure is thus broader and different from spatial proportion or spatial form.

Many architects have looked to rules and systems for support in establishing the proportions of rooms. Why? Part of the answer is given by Le Corbusier in his article 'L'architecture et l'esprit mathématique', in which he analyses several of his early facade sketches:

The arbitrariness of the openings in the facade makes my eyes hurt; I fill them in with charcoal and those black smudges speak a language, but their language is incoherent. The absence of a rule, a law makes my eyes hurt; dejected, I can only assert that I am working in total chaos.[23]

Systematizing and organizing our impressions in order to avoid working in what Le Corbusier called 'design chaos' is one explanation for the widespread use of systems of proportion to generate form.

History

An important aspect of spatial figure is the relationship between a room's length, breadth and height – its proportions. The word proportion stems from the Latin *proportio*, which means 'relating to' or 'of uniform measure'. Artistic proportions were formulated by the Pythagorean philosophers, who categorized dimensional conditions based on the relationships among various tonal intervals in music. They compared the lengths of various strings and the tone each produced to building dimensions and the perceived beauty resulting from those dimensions.

One of the eldest and most well-known descriptions of a proportional system is Vitruvius' *Ten Books of Architecture*. The rediscovery of Vitruvius in the fifteenth century provided the basis for a number of methods of proportioning developed during the Renaissance, including Alberti's *Ten Books of Architecture* (1485) and

Villa Rotonda, Andrea Palladio.

Palladio's *Four Books of Architecture* (1570). In Book Nine, Alberti suggests that for each room form there is an appropriate function and size. Square shapes should be used for smaller rooms, for example, and rectangular shapes for larger. Exemplary proportions for rectangular spaces were 2:3 or 3:5, approximating the 'Golden Section'. Alberti recommends a ceiling height equal to the average of a room's length and width, thereby mathematically connecting the height of a space with its plan form.

Renaissance systems of proportion are characterized by the notion that certain proportions are invested with inherent beauty. Proportional systems were seen as a kind of manual for producing beauty and determining the perception of a space in advance. The balanced tranquillity of Renaissance space was replaced by movement and contrast during the Mannerist and Baroque eras. Despite changes in expression, the architectural vocabulary was still based on Classical traditions.

The Enlightenment of the eighteenth century brought a shift in the way people viewed the concept of beauty. Many questioned the absolute connection between systems of proportion and beauty in architecture. Instead, a more subjective notion of aesthetic qualities developed, and it became possible to apply rules and proportions more individually. Architects were to combine a selection of properly proportioned parts to create a harmonious whole.

Methods of proportioning played a prominent role in the education of architects through the nineteenth century, when there were handbooks that catalogued the proportions of architecture.

The new ideas in housing that came to light at the close of the nineteenth century, influenced by the Arts and Crafts Movement, diminished the use and relevance of the rules and systems of proportioning developed during the Renaissance. The Arts and Crafts Movement emphasized the importance of craftsmanship and free artistic creativity. Dynamic composition and the accommodation of site characteristics were now important aspects of residential design. John Ruskin, one of the movement's most prominent theorists, had great disdain for the rule systems used by architects, and advocated a new architecture that would gather inspiration from natural forms rather than Renaissance rules. He found historical precedent for such an approach in Gothic architecture, which he saw as emanating from actual practical requirements, and free from the restrictions of suffocating laws.

Liberation from systems of rules allowed architects to design more freely, though their work continued to rely on a basic knowledge of the Classical vocabulary.

Housing plans, inspired by the early Arts and Crafts Movement, changed the way the rooms of the traditional home were organized. Rooms were now frequently oriented outward to face a garden or a beautiful view, giving the home a deeper relationship to its site. At the start of the twentieth century the new ideas even began to affect the form of individual rooms. The principal rooms of Charles Voysey's homes from the first years of the century were divided and articulated to provide more intimate niches within the larger space; there was often a fireplace nook, a bay window facing the view, and places for contact with adjoining rooms.

Modernism and Functionalism added new aspects to the generation of spatial figure. Standard dimensions for space planning and various functions were developed through a programme of housing research, and these dimensional standards had a powerful influence on the design of apartments.

Many architects saw construction standardization as the future solution to the problem of housing design. The development of correctly planned standards was thought to ensure a higher quality of housing. Standardization was considered a necessity for lowering construction costs and increasing the pace of production. When the functionally optimal dimensions and furnishing requirements that came out of housing research were tied to active national housing policies, they began to control residential architecture.

Design systems

In 1945, immediately following the end of the Second World War, Le Corbusier presented a new system of proportion he called 'Le Modulor'. His interest in systems of proportion was influenced by industrial production methods. Le Corbusier was dissatisfied with the French authorities' standardization efforts and the development of Le Modulor was a proposal for a more suitable and harmonious set of standards. He saw the system as a means of achieving a certain architectural quality: 'The power of numbers, master of proportions. Proportions: dispensers of harmony, of smiles, of graces and nobility, in things that are built'.[24]

Another system of proportion from about the same time as Le Modulor is the 'Plastic Number', developed by Dutch architect and Benedictine monk Dom Hans van der Laan.[25] The Plastic Number provides a framework for dividing lines, surfaces and spaces. It uses the thickness of a wall as the point of departure for a building's proportions. The ideal relationship between wall thickness and room width in van der Laan's system is 1:7. This width then determines the height and size of the room, its openings and its window sizes. A common recommendation for a room's length-to-width proportions is 3:4. The importance of the wall is reflected in its function as a border and dividing line between the exterior space of nature and the interior space of experience. Van der Laan's dimensional series is built on intervals between threshold values, and has many practical similarities to the Golden Section and Le Modulor.

Van der Laan asserts that the Plastic Number works like an objective measuring scale that has similarities to music's various tonal scales. The principal design task for the architect is then to determine the relationships among these scales. The dimensions themselves – the frequencies of the tones – are predetermined elements of the system. The sum of the first and second numbers

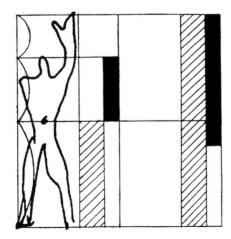

Le Modulor, Le Corbusier.

is the fourth number, the sum of the second and third is the fifth, and so on. The first number is equal to the difference between the fifth and sixth numbers. The point of departure for each measurement is the centre-line of a wall. Lines, surfaces and rooms can be proportioned after the values derived from the Plastic Number.

Rooms of the postwar housing boom conform to specific types with little divergence, their areas given by standard minimum dimensions: the half-room of 7m² (75 sq ft), the smaller bedroom of 10m² (108 sq ft), the larger bedroom of 12m² (129 sq ft), and the living room of 18–20m² (194–215 sq ft).

Many architects have investigated the significance of spatial figure in our experience of architecture, and discussion on the subject seems never to cease. During the 1940s and 1950s, functional utility was even incorporated into aesthetic guidelines and theories of proportion. In 1957, British architects met under the auspices of the Royal Institute of British Architects (RIBA) to discuss the advantages and disadvantages of using systems of proportion. After a vote they determined that such systems do not facilitate 'good design'.

The interest in systematic design seems to have been often intertwined with attempts to find the forms that are most pleasing to people. I have never found any

Benedictine monastery outside Tomelilla, Sweden, opened in 1991 and designed by Van der Laan in strict compliance with the 'Plastic Number'.

empirical evidence to demonstrate the superiority of the Golden Section or any other proportional relations. Nevertheless there is a strong tradition of forming space after certain proportions. A comparison between modern residential spaces and the proportions advocated during the Renaissance, for example, shows a striking similarity.

Daylight

'In any image, where there is space there is light.'[26] The implications of this quotation extend from the

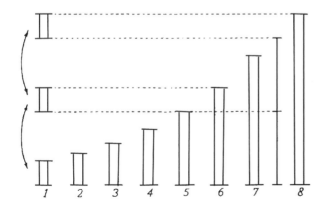

The 'Plastic Number', Van der Laan. The sum of the second and third numbers is the fourth. The sum of the third and fourth numbers is the fifth, and so on. The first number is equal to the difference between the fifth and sixth numbers.

fundamental importance of daylight in our perception of architecture to the mysterious and inconceivable aspects of the presence of light in the home:

> The architect can fix the dimensions of solids and cavities, he can designate the orientation of his building, he can specify the materials and the way they are to be treated, he can describe precisely the quantities and qualities he desires in his building before a stone has been laid. Daylight alone he cannot control. It changes from morning to evening, from day to day, both in intensity and colour. How is it possible to work with such a capricious factor?[27]

Rasmussen illuminates the difficulty of describing both the measurable and non-measurable attributes of daylighting in the home. At the same time, the quotation above gives an idea of all the design possibilities available to an architect in working with natural light.

The historical development of daylight in the home

Our spatial experience is often tied to various historical lighting archetypes and atmospheres, for example we often associate light from above with a sacred and mystical mood. Toplighting can be found as early as the basilica form of the first Christian churches. Light from above was used to highlight the choir and accentuate the pulpit within the space of the sanctuary. This concept was fully developed in Gothic architecture, with high stained-glass clerestory windows that filled cathedrals with a spiritual and mystical light.

Illuminating a space from below was, at least until the introduction of electric light, associated with the theatre: 'This sort of illumination became a convention of the theatre, and when the footlights went on they immediately created that atmosphere of enchantment, an unreality which is the world of the stage'.[28]

The relationship between daylight strategies and residential architecture has undergone a long historical development. A smoke hole in the roof was the only source of daylight throughout the earlier periods of history. The first facade openings for light were small holes with sliding shutters. The original meaning of the word 'window' derives from holes in the facade for air and wind.[29] Glass was expensive and the first windows were therefore limited in size.

Technical improvements in the production of glass during the nineteenth century steadily increased the size of windows used in homes. The development of glass technology was an important element in the new type of home that emerged in Europe at the end of the century. Previously deep and dark apartments were

Light from above. San Giorgio Maggiore, Venice. Andrea Palladio, begun in 1566.

brightened by the addition of glazed-over courtyards at the heart of the building block. Daylight took on the new role of defining the centre of a building and gathering other elements around itself, both physically and aesthetically. One of the most prominent figures of the time, Belgian architect Victor Horta, often placed a top-lit stairwell at the heart of the home.

A wealth of daylight was an important aspect of the Functionalist home developed in the 1920s and 1930s. The well-lit home was a reaction to, and a symbolic liberation from, the previously sun-deprived courtyard apartment. Light-filled and cross-ventilated apartments were seen as promoting better hygiene and therefore inhibiting disease. Methods were soon developed for calculating the daylight in the home.

Meanwhile, Functionalism brought a change in the traditional method of leading daylight into the home. Developments in construction methods made obsolete the traditional pattern of vertically oriented window openings flanked on either side by load-bearing masonry walls. These were replaced in the new Functionalist architecture by the horizontal ribbon window. Le Corbusier extolled the virtues of the ribbon window, which he said made more of the view by opening up a horizontal panorama. Those who advocated the vertically oriented window, including August Perret, claimed that it let light deeper into the interior because of its lower sill and included more of the bright light from high in the sky due to its greater height.

Functionalism also had an impact on the design of the window. The moulded frame and sash was replaced by a rectangular section. Heavier glass with better thermo-insulation characteristics required stronger windows. The moulded sash increased at the expense of the glazed opening. The result was darker homes. An important prerequisite was thereby lost for the articulation of the incoming daylight. The rich play of light and shadow that characterized the window with moulded frame and sash was replaced by a simplified refraction of light over smooth, rectangular details.

All of these developments led to darker apartments.

A top-lit stairwell at the heart of the home. Hotel Tassel, Brussels. Victor Horta 1893–95. © 1999 Victor Horta – SOFAM – Belgium.

Throughout the 1990s, daylight has played an increasingly prominent role in architecture, while technological developments have improved the insulating capacity and light transmittance of glass. Prominent architects such as Rem Koolhaas, Jean Nouvel and Henning Larsen have designed buildings in which natural light and openness are fundamental to the expression of the architecture and to our perception of it. One unifying factor is an interest in giving expression to the penetration of light from outside into the interior space. Modernism's use of entirely glazed walls

A boundary can be interpreted. The art gallery, Malmö Konsthall. Architect Klas Anselm.

The BT building, Copenhagen. Architect: Henning Larsen, 1994. Night and day photographs. A screen of perforated steel gives the facade different characteristics by day and by night.

in striving for immateriality has been complemented by the addition of transparent layers that in a variety of ways delay the passage of light between inside and out, giving the interior a veiled and enigmatic character. As daylight is caught in the layers of material that make up the facade, the boundary between interior and exterior space is dispersed. In the multi-layered glass walls of Jean Nouvel's Cartier Foundation in Paris, the reflections in the extra glazing prevent passers by from seeing directly into the interior.[30] Henning Larsen achieves a similar effect in an office building in central Copenhagen by exploiting the double aspects of a screen – transparency and surface.

Attributes of daylight in the home

A few of the many attributes of daylight in the home can be measured and regulated. One of these measurable attributes is the indoor daylight factor – the ratio of daylight illumination at a point inside to the illuminance outside under an unobstructed sky. Another attribute that can be quantified is the amount of illuminance from direct sunlight in each room of the home, which depends on its orientation.

Glare is more difficult to measure. Lighting contrast varies on a scale from a comfortable brightness ratio to blinding glare. If direct sunlight can be diffused, and the transition between the contrasting interior and exterior illuminance softened, then the risk of glare is reduced. Traditional methods of moderating this contrast in brightness include the use of light-coloured translucent curtains, splayed window embrasures that reflect daylight, moulded sash and frame, and pale colours in the transition zone between inside and out.

It is unpleasant to look out through a 'straight' window made from square-sectional pieces – you get a glare between inside and out. One method of softening the glare is to insert some form of tracery, like glazing bars and mullions, that is illuminated from the side. That's one method; there may be others.

That's why we perceive the windows at Västra Kungshall [Case study Stumholmen] as pleasant and gratifying, because this mild contrast feels good to the eye.[31]

'It is unpleasant to look out through a "straight" window made from square-sectional pieces – you get a glare between inside and out. One method of softening the glare is to insert some form of tracery, like glazing bars and mullions, that is illuminated from the side. That's one method: There may be others. That's why we perceive the windows at Västra Kungshall as pleasant and gratifying, because this mild contrast feels good to the eye'. Quote from an interview with Kjell Forshed – see Chapter 4, 'Case study Stumholmen'. Photograph from Stumholmen, Karlskrona. Photo: Sten Gromark.

These glare-reducing features create a kind of imaginary room within the room, a transitional space filled with diffuse daylight. As Sven Hesselgren notes: 'The more gradual and the more articulated that transition, the smaller the daylight factor can be before there is glare'.[32]

The window niches in Hammershöi's scenes seem filled with light reflected from the window's frame, sash and side panels. Rays of direct sunlight pierce through this glow. The combination of soft reflected light and sharp direct light produces a third condition of intense light with a dense and concentrated character. Hammershöi makes clear the path of the sunlight as it enters the room and reflects from the floor. *Støvkornenes dans i solstrålerne*. Vilhelm Hammershöi, 1900. © 1999 Ordrupgaard, Copenhagen.

Non-measurable daylight factors include top-lighting, reflected light, shadow patterns, illuminance levels and lighting distribution. What determines the character of a space is not the number or quantity of these factors, but rather their relationship to one another and to the space. Past research has indicated that the integrating and clarifying effect of daylight can be charted by monitoring reflected surfaces, illuminance levels, illuminance distribution, shadow formation and modelling conditions.

The paintings of Jan Vermeer, a Dutch artist of the seventeenth century, provide an elegant depiction of how light enters into a Northern European dwelling through a traditional window. There is typically a person standing at a window that admits a soft light, modelling the objects within, a necessary condition for the handiwork, letter-writing or confidential conversation taking place in the room. Vermeer's paintings illustrate the way reflected light casts soft shadows. On occasion he paints a more conventionally side-lit space in which the direct lighting casts sharp shadows.

Danish painter Vilhelm Hammershöi (1864–1916) made similar observations of daylight in domestic spaces. His paintings illustrate the play of light and shadow over the moulded details of a window. The window niches in Hammershöi's scenes seem filled with light reflected from the window's frame, sash and side panels. Rays of direct sunlight pierce through this glow. The combination of soft reflected light and sharp direct light produces a third condition of intense light with a dense and concentrated character. Hammershöi makes clear the path of the sunlight as it enters the room and reflects from the floor, its eventful movement contrasting with the stillness of the room.

The play of light in the window accentuates the symbolic expanse of a hole in the wall, according to lighting expert Anders Liljefors: 'The brighter areas work like magnets if they are contrasted by darker surroundings … A darker or brighter patch that appears within an otherwise contrast-free field captures our attention immediately. Our eyes are thus attracted

Illustration from Armand Björkman, *Skisser och sånt* (Sketches and similar things), p. 93, Gothenburg, 1988. Björkman shows an apartment designed by Gaudi with a fivefold increase in depth in which each room has its own light characteristics, clearly and consistently distinct from its neighbours.

to the light if it can be compared to something darker … The brightest surfaces should convey meaningful information'.[33]

A window niche and the light it captures tell something of the relationship between the private space of the interior and the public space outside. The inside surface of the wall is in shadow – lit only indirectly by light reflected back from the interior of the room. The contrast in brightness between window niche and wall surface accentuates the difference between aperture and surround.

Another way of designing with daylight is to work with differences in light among the various rooms and areas of a home. In the narrow and extremely deep apartments of the European continent, interior partitions are often used as surfaces for gathering light. As a result, certain rooms are lit at the expense of others. The central hall in many continental apartments is a dim, indirectly lit space flanked by brighter rooms along the street and courtyard. A room with windows on two sides has mixed lighting conditions, with bright modelling light near the windows and softer modelling light near the middle of the space.

In summary, our historical survey reveals an increasing interest in the non-measurable attributes of daylight. We can distinguish a growing demand for a qualitative treatment of daylight to complement the quantitative requirements that guided the design of the Functionalist apartment. The design and detailing of windows, as well as the niches in which they are placed, determine the character of daylight in the home.

Organization of spaces

The organization of rooms is the arrangement of the home's private interior space and of its public exterior space, and the relationship between these two. The organization of the home's rooms has gone through major changes in the past 150 years.

The middle-class home of the nineteenth century was characterized by its large rooms, the ability to walk a circuit through the apartment, an arrangement of spaces in parallel bands, and axial circulation paths. The part of the apartment dedicated to formal entertaining included a semi-private area. Worker housing, on the other hand, had general rooms that could be utilized for a variety of purposes. The interface between interior and exterior spaces in these apartments provided a finely tuned series of territorial boundaries.

The Functionalist apartment was made up of differentiated and functionally determinate rooms. The provision for a neutral circulation hub was critical since, in these small apartments, every room might be used as a bedroom.

The relationship between home and site changed radically in the urban developments of the Functionalist era. The ideal urban space moved towards a more diffuse environment in which buildings were sited to maximize their exposure to the sun and to make the

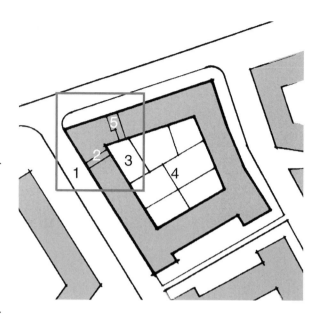

A sequence of space:
1 the street,
2 the portal,
3 the little courtyard,
4 the great courtyard space,
5 the stairwell and
the individual apartment.

most of the given features of the natural landscape. The open spaces between buildings offered less opportunity for residents to establish a sense of territoriality. During the 1960s and 1970s, the size of both apartments and housing developments increased. The vast scope of these developments made it hard for residents to become familiar with their neighbourhoods or define their own territory. Insensitive landscaping made such territoriality less appealing and more difficult. As a whole, the public environment offered inhabitants little incentive to compete for or defend territory.

During the 1960s and 1970s, a standardized form emerged for the Functionalist apartment. It had functionally differentiated rooms, standardized room sizes, a radial circulation pattern of rooms surrounding and entered from a neutral hall, and a well-planned scheme with easy accessibility.

Boundary – wall of stone.

important support in the process of appropriation. Eva Hurtig demonstrates in her research the importance of the connection between the home and its site. A meaningful home life requires that the individual is able to establish a relationship to the home. Territory is a way for us to create identity, orient ourselves within a place, and feel at home.[36]

Residents can complete the appropriation process in successive stages if the grounds around their apartment building are given varying degrees of privacy. One outdoor space at a time can be added to the private, secure territory of the home. Clear boundaries between

Establishing territory

An important aspect of the organization of spaces is giving residents an opportunity to stake out territory within the public space adjoining the home. Territory is defined by *The Oxford Dictionary of English Etymology* as 'Land belonging to a town, a ruler or state'.[34]

Territoriality used to be considered something that applied only to animals. The idea that human beings also establish territory is a relatively new concept. Torsten Malmberg's comprehensive work *Räkna med revir* (Count on Territory, 1983) was an early study on the subject. According to Malmberg, human territory can be manifested at a variety of sizes and scales: 'A territory can be a chair, but it can also be the planet we inhabit'.[35] His definition of territoriality is built on eight keywords: territoriality is the awareness of a certain area by a particular group, control over that area by the group, the reservation of the area exclusively for the group, and the delineation and marking of the area by the group. There must also be competition for the area with others and an opportunity to defend it. Together these elements create an identity relationship between a group and its territory.

The combination of the rooms inside the home and the design of the space that surrounds it can provide an

Meeting between house and its surroundings. Summer house, Varberg.

'It is first and foremost through identification with a place that we adapt our lives to a particular form of existence . . . Thus dwelling means above all becoming acquainted with something, becoming tied to something'. Christian Norberg-Schulz, *Mellom jord og himmel* (Between Heaven and Earth, in Norwegian only), p. 88, Oslo, 1978.

these spaces allow residents to mark territory. By sharing responsibility for the maintenance of a courtyard or some other part of the site, residents demonstrate control over their territory. They mark this territory by personalizing it with plantings and other landscaping elements. The presence of historical remnants and patterns can also aid in the process of appropriation. A harmonious social system provides opportunities for individuals to meet others and socialize, but also to be alone.

A good relationship between the home and its surroundings is essential to a meaningful home life. A prerequisite is that the individual first be able to establish a relationship to the home. Territoriality is a method of creating identity, of allowing an individual to orient him- or herself on the site and to feel at home.

Architecture has a greater influence over daily life than many realize or are willing to admit. The goal of appropriation is to give identity to the home, to establish a relationship between residents, the home and its surrounding site. The home is the starting point for feelings of territoriality and identification in the exterior public realm. 'The ultimate meaning of architecture is to give our existence content . . . The process of appropriation enables a person to conceive of him-self as capable of assigning significance, meaning and importance to the rooms and places he inhabits or visits . . . Collective appropriation is a matter of architecture'.[37]

An important part of appropriation is residents' participation in various neighbourhood processes. Architectural scholar Tage Wiklund outlines a wide framework for these processes. While Mediterranean cities keep nature at an 'urban distance', Scandinavians choose to live in cities only of necessity – nature remains the ideal. For Scandinavians, a home's relationship to nature is an important part of its value: 'A Nordic building opens to its surroundings at the same time it is woven into them'.[38] Wiklund asserts that while Mediterranean city-dwellers relate to nature as observers, the inhabitants of Scandinavian cities are participants in nature.

The relationship between a home and its site cannot be measured – it is part of a poetic relationship to reality. According to Norberg-Schulz: 'To dwell means to respect one's surroundings – to befriend them. We can never be friends with data . . . Friendship has to do with qualities'.[39] Dwelling is not a world apart from the space of nature that surrounds the home, but rather a world in which the home and its site are united, 'an "interior" that is in harmony with its exterior'.[40]

The ability to identify with one's house, with one's dwelling, is thus critically important:

> It is first and foremost through identification with a place that we adapt our lives to a particular form of existence . . . Thus dwelling means above all becoming acquainted with something, becoming tied to something.[41]

Architecture can ensure the continuation of local traditions and make the prior history of a place part of the new inhabitant's identity.

In summary, the organization of spaces includes the prerequisites for our identification with the public space of the city or the natural landscape that surrounds the home. Architecture can either enhance or inhibit the process of appropriation by which residents establish a sense of home – a process that is inevitably necessary. The organization of spaces in the home is part of our interpretation of the site – of the meeting between the resident, the home and its natural surroundings – and is of great importance to our perception of the architecture of the home.

The home should help us form a meaningful interpretation of the spirit of the site, or what Norberg-Schultz calls 'genius loci'. There must be a meaningful relationship between a resident, his or her home and the surrounding site. Only then can the resident make these rooms and this place his or her own – only then can he or she make of them a home.

Lighthouse on the Ven island.

Chapter 4

Case studies

This chapter deals with the question, 'What forms do the non-measurable architectural attributes of the home take?'. It presents four case studies in which I have evaluated the relevance of the fields of attributes previously identified. The chapter describes the architecture in each of the cases using the concepts and theoretical framework developed during the process of identification. These attributes and concepts have served as tools and approaches with which to treat the empirical material. Identification and analysis have in many cases proceeded in parallel. During the course of my work with each case study I discovered important architectural attributes. I have also used the case studies to evaluate the relevance of various concepts and theories to a characterization of the perception of residential architecture.

Although the four examples in the case studies are located in Sweden, they demonstrate attributes that apply throughout the world.

The account of each case study incorporates quotations from my interviews with residents and architects. The purpose of these quotations is to give a more intimate portrayal of how the architecture of the home is perceived by the residents I met, and to enrich the studies with the insights into housing design of the projects' architects. All the residents interviewed remain anonymous. For the sake of legibility I have given them all new names.

The case studies are arranged in the chronological order in which they were conducted:

Case study Lindholmen is a one-bedroom apartment built in 1992 in the Lindholmen district of Gothenburg. It covers 69m² (743 sq ft). and was designed by Armand Björkman of White arkitekter.

Case study Stumholmen is a two-bedroom apartment built in 1993 on the island of Stumholmen in Karlskrona. It covers 82m² (883 sq ft) and was designed by Kjell Forshed of Brunnberg & Forshed Arkitektkontor.

Case study Hestra includes several apartments in the Nielsen block of the Hestra development in the town of Borås that were built in 1992–3. The architect was Jens Thomas Arnfred of the Danish firm Vandkunstens Tegnestue.

Case study Norrköping includes two- and three-bedroom apartments in the Vattenkonsten block in Norrköping, built in 1987 and designed by Bengt Lindroos. Each has an area of 98m² (1,055 sq ft).

Case study Lindholmen

Description
Case study Lindholmen covers several one-bedroom duplex apartments in the Lindholmen district of Gothenburg, designed by Armand Björkman of White arkitekter. The development was completed in 1992.

The ground floor is occupied by the one-bedroom 69m² (743 sq ft) units included in the case study, while the second and third floors hold two-level three-bedroom units. There are four apartments per stairwell, two on each level.

The apartments are divided into three longitudinal chains of rooms – along the courtyard, along the street and through the middle. The courtyard side of the apartment is thereby separated from the street side, a prerequisite for the division of the apartment into

View of both of the newly built blocks.

different zones for privacy and activity. Off to the side somewhat lies a work zone comprising the kitchen and laundry room. The bedroom opens to the living room and faces the courtyard, and is the apartment's most private area. The living room and dining area are for socializing.

The new buildings are located on two blocks bounded by Lindholmsvägen to the south and Släggaregatan to the north, Verkmästaregatan to the east and Plåtslagaregatan to the west. The grade slopes several feet from the north end of the lot down towards the southwest. The development includes eleven freestanding buildings with four apartments each, and two longer buildings with eight each – a total of 60 apartments. The buildings surround a long and narrow courtyard divided into smaller spaces by outbuildings. The smaller four-unit buildings are 9 × 18.6m (29.5 × 61 ft) with two storeys plus an attic and no basement level. The facades are clad in moulded vertical woodsiding. The courtyard elevation has an entrance veranda flanked on either side by bay windows.

The district of Lindholmen occupies a promontory overlooking the inner harbour of Gothenburg, about a hundred metres (328 ft) from the northern bank of the Göta River. The area has a long history, its name having been found in written documents as early as 1253, with the mention of Lindholmen Castle. Its more recent history is intimately tied to the founding, growth and eventual demise of Lindholmen Shipyard. Established in 1854, the shipyard expanded rapidly. By the 1880s it employed 2,000 workers, making it one of the region's largest workplaces. At the time of the First World War, Lindholmen had nearly 5,000 inhabitants.

The district fell into economic decline in the 1960s, and when the shipyard closed in 1977 Lindholmen was in a wretched state of disrepair. Buildings were vandalized, with some occupied by drug addicts. In the 1980s, a comprehensive renovation of the neighbourhood was undertaken, and many of the buildings were remodelled by resident groups. The municipal government announced plans to build new units as a

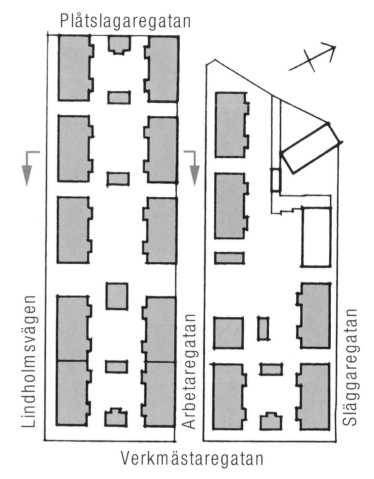

Plåtslagaregatan

Lindholmsvägen

Arbetaregatan

Släggaregatan

Verkmästaregatan

Site layout of the two newly built blocks.
New buildings are marked in grey.

complement to renovation efforts. The housing development in this case study was part of this initiative.

The organization of spaces in the Lindholmen apartments differs in several respects from the standard Functionalist home: one can walk a circuit around the dimly lit core, as previously mentioned the apartment is divided longitudinally, some rooms are accessible only through living spaces, and the buildings have a meaningful relationship to the site.

I first visited these buildings in 1994 as part of a postgraduate course. Together with a colleague, I interviewed a couple of tenants at that time. We developed

Courtyard facade.

voiced their appreciation for the design of the courtyard, its open expanse carved with clear territorial boundaries. These carefully conceived boundaries offer exciting opportunities for interpretation.

Case study Lindholmen was undertaken in the spring of 1995. My aim was to study apartments of varying sizes and on opposite sides of the courtyard. I interviewed the residents of six apartments over the course of four evenings. The buildings' architects, Armand Björkman and Ursel Mattsson of White arkitekter, collaborated with me on these interviews.

I have limited the case study here to the one-bedroom schemes, the plan of which is repeated on the lower level of the three-bedroom units. The upper level of these larger apartments is therefore not illustrated. The tenant interviewees of the one-bedroom units were an elderly couple and two young couples, one with a small child. In the larger apartments, the interviewees were a single mother with a teenage child, another single mother with small children, and a middle-aged couple. In June of 1995 I interviewed Armand Björkman about his intentions for the design work on the project.

a positive impression from these first introductory visits to the project, coloured by residents' obvious appreciation of their homes. I was impressed by elements such as the working kitchen, the adjacent well-lit and open dining area, and the hall. I found the organization of spaces and the contact between the apartments and the courtyard deftly executed and exciting. Residents

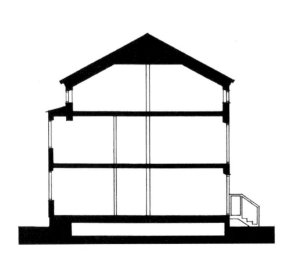

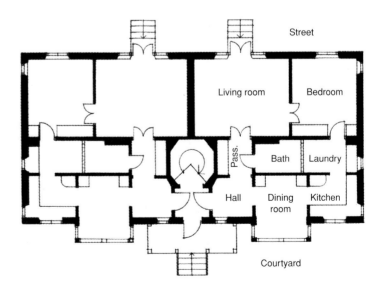

Entry level with two apartments and section. Scale 1:200.

The Lindholmen study helped me identify the field of attributes I call *organization of spaces*. Outdoor spaces were consciously and clearly designed with territorial markings and boundaries. In the interviews, both residents and the architects talked about territory and boundaries in the organization of spaces. The field of attributes was consolidated in studies of literature that included the work of Johan Asplund and Karl-Olov Arnstberg on the concepts *Gemeinschaft* and *Gesellschaft*.

Later in my work, the Lindholmen apartment also helped identify the *movement* field of attributes. The layout of the apartment clearly provides the conditions for a variety of movements.

Materials and detailing

The materials and detailing at Lindholmen exemplify the typical standard of their day. The floors on the street side are hardwood, with linoleum throughout the rest of the apartment. The walls are papered and the smooth ceilings painted white. The trim around windows and doors is factory-painted with butt joints rather than the traditional mitred corners. The glossed casement windows open inward, their frame and sash subtly moulded. The sides of the window niches are splayed. A wall of glass block separates bathroom and laundry room.

Few of the tenants interviewed commented on the materials of their apartments, though one was somewhat critical:

> We looked at a model apartment, but I backed out almost immediately. I thought the surface of everything was plasticky. There was a lot of fake wood, and I didn't think much of the closets, either.
>
> (Personal interview (Johan), Johan and Jenny, one-bedroom apartment residents)

Many of those interviewed appreciated the glass block between the bathroom and laundry. Frida recounted:

> I think they're quite fun. Even if it isn't entirely necessary, it's still pretty nice to have them. They let in a little light during the day.
>
> (Personal interview, Frida, three-bedroom apartment resident)

However, there are generally few materials or details that indicate particular care or authenticity, or that were mentioned by tenants. The materials and detailing of these apartments thus play a subsidiary role in residents' perception of their homes.

Axiality

Paths and sightlines connect the rooms of the Lindholmen apartment with one another. From one room the lighting conditions and atmosphere of others can be observed. Axiality makes the apartment 'surveyable', that is it can be taken in at a glance. Axial directions and paths also influence how one moves through and perceives possibilities for movement through the rooms of the apartment.

The apartment has four architectural axes. The two main axes are encountered in the entrance hall. A transverse axis extends from the hall through the passageway, through the living room to a window area and a patio door or a shallow balcony. The longitudinal main axis extends from the hall through an opening into the dining area, then through a second opening into the kitchen where it ends at a small square window.

The origin of the transverse axis is the hall, and its goal is the windows and door towards the courtyard, two of the important points of the apartment. The axis integrates three rooms through broad openings – a flat archway between hall and passageway, and glazed French doors between the passageway and the living room. The rooms differ in form, material and size. The length of the main transverse axis, the number of rooms it penetrates, the size of the openings between them and the importance of its start- and endpoints all give it great dignity.

The laundry room and the bedroom
from the kitchen.

Transverse primary axis, view of the passage and hallway
from the living room.

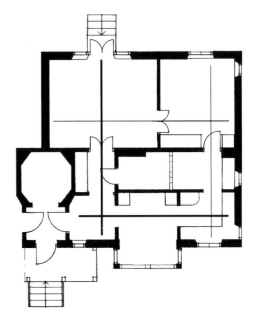

The axiality of the apartment. Primary axes and
secondary axes. Scale 1:200.

The primary longitudinal axis is illuminated by daylight as it extends through three rooms along the façade, experiencing different daylight conditions. The rooms are interconnected through two broad archways, and are asymmetrically placed about the axis. The start- and endpoints of the longitudinal axis are significant points. The bright daylight of the dining area and its opening towards the courtyard inspire a movement along the axis. Elsa remembers the kitchen's dining area from her first visit to the apartment: 'I don't know what it was that made up my mind about the apartment. I think I fell for this kitchen' (personal interview: Elsa, one-bedroom apartment resident).

Two secondary axes complement the two primary axes. One is transverse, crossing from the kitchen through the laundry room to the bedroom; the other runs longitudinally, connecting the living room and bedroom. The apartment's dim central core obscures the secondary axes from the entrance. We notice them first as we move along one of the main axes. The secondary axes are less dignified due to their smaller openings and less significant start- and endpoints.

Enclosure

Spatial openness and enclosure are important aspects of the relationship between the apartment and the court-yard, between the home and its site, and between the personal space of experience and the surrounding space of nature. The apartment contains both open and closed rooms. On the courtyard side, the kitchen, dining area and hall have a more open character than the bedroom and living room on the street side. The spatial enclosure of the street-side rooms is generated by clearly legible room forms. Details such as distinct corners, small openings in wall surfaces, doorway thresholds and headers over windows and doors make these rooms easy to read. This enclosure is accentuated in the living room by the bilateral symmetry of the opening to the hall with the window to the street.

The openness of the courtyard side of the apartment depends largely on the wide openings between the

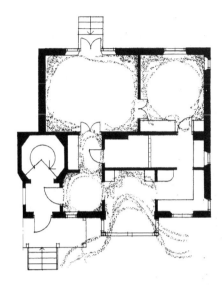

Enclosure of the apartment, marked in heavy lines.
Scale 1:200

rooms and the dining area's bay window on to the courtyard. The absence of thresholds here emphasizes the spatial interaction between rooms. Harriet talked about the openness of her home:

> Well, they see in, you know – even more than we do, actually, since they're looking down at us. Sometimes it doesn't matter, but sometimes you feel like it's not okay.
>
> (Personal interview, Harriet and Harry, one-bedroom apartment residents)

Several details articulate the boundaries between rooms, including window headers, the corner posts in the bay window, and small partial walls between the dining area, the working part of the kitchen and the hall. These help consolidate the relationship between open and closed and between interior and exterior space. The openness of the dining area is of great importance in connecting apartment and courtyard, as well as fostering contact between residents.

The perception of security in the interior rooms of the apartment is a prerequisite to the appropriation

View of the dining room from the kitchen.

Movement

Several types of movement are possible in the Lindholmen apartment. One can walk a circuit from one room to another around the dimly lit central core, or walk along the axial paths that play a prominent role in our perception of the apartment. For the architect, there were various aspects to the circuit movement:

> Our idea was to create a feeling of spaciousness within the limited area of a one-bedroom apartment by making it possible to walk in a circle. The passageway between kitchen and bedroom is part of that possibility. Of course you can close the door if you want. Those who don't want it to be open can always put a bookcase or something in front of the door. If we had instead put a wall there, no one would have cut a door in it. And then there might be family situations in which, for example, the woman of the house wants to use the living room for entertaining just her friends while the man retires to the bedroom, and he can in fact go in and out through that door. Or in the case of a single parent with a teenage child, the living room can be used as a bedroom, and the passage through the laundry room means you don't have to walk through one bedroom to get to the other.
>
> (Personal interview, Armand Björkman, architect)

of the space outside. In the dining area's bay window, the apartment's interior symbolically penetrates the outside wall, establishing contact with the exterior. The open dining area occupies the border between the private sphere of the interior and the public sphere of the exterior.

The design of an interior space can focus our attention on important elements of the space outside, thus aiding the process of appropriation. Openness and enclosure can be used to prepare us for the discovery of exterior conditions.

This circulation loop interconnects the apartment's three longitudinal parts – the street side, the courtyard side and the central zone between them. The circuit movement thus reveals the contrast between courtyard and street, between the semi-private atmosphere of the courtyard and the public character of the street space. It also increases the apartment's flexibility and enriches our perception of the place by adding paths and sight-lines from room to room. In three of the six apartments visited, the residents had chosen to close off this circuit. Elsa and Erik had the door sealed to allow them greater latitude in furnishing the apartment:

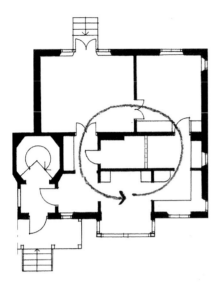

Circulation loop.
Scale 1:200.

cross: the small rooms can be read quickly as we pass through them, while the larger living room requires more time for surveying and orientation. As we slow down in the larger rooms, our movement takes on a rhythm given by spatial form.

There is a different rhythm along the longitudinal axis. The greater size and abundance of daylight make the dining area a natural goal for movements from the smaller and darker hall and kitchen. The dining area is the Lindholmen apartment's *border space*. Entering from the stairwell, the visitor is already pointed in the

We took out the door in there and made a whole wall instead. There was no need for that door between the bedroom and the laundry room. We called in during construction, and we got a wall we can use both on this side and the other.

> (Personal interview, Elsa and Erik, one-bedroom apartment residents)

For Harriet and Harry, however, the circuit opportunity was a valuable asset:

It makes it more free somehow, because otherwise the bedroom is too separated from the rest – that's how we feel anyway.

> (Personal interview, Harriet and Harry, one-bedroom apartment residents)

Daylight illuminates the apartment along its axial paths. We are drawn towards the brightly lit rooms along the facade, moving through the darker middle of the apartment along the axes. Daylight is the goal of our movements between the two facades. The speed of these movements varies with the size of the space we

Rooms on the courtyard side, view of dining room and kitchen from the hallway.

are received in the hall and invited to sit down in the dining area.

Spatial figure

The spatial figures of the Lindholmen apartment coincide in many ways with the typical spaces of the standard Functionalist apartment. Its largest room is the 20m² (215 sq ft) living room. It has two medium-sized rooms – the 12m² (129 sq ft) bedroom and the 8m² (86 sq ft) dining area. The remaining rooms are small, with areas of 3 to 5m² (32–54 sq ft).

The apartment's plan form is nearly square. It is divided longitudinally into two halves of equal depth by a wall between street side and the middle area. Its smaller rooms have similar proportions to its larger rooms. The three main spaces – living room, bedroom and dining area – have a descending proportional relationship each to the next of 3:2, the bedroom having half again the area of the dining room, with the living room larger still by half.

The kitchen, passageway, laundry room and bathroom are small spaces with built-in furnishings and it is thus difficult to evaluate the perception of spatial figure in these.

View from Verkmästaregatan street.

direction of the light-filled bay window. For Jenny the dining area made an important first impression. She told me: 'Well I thought it was cozy to have a dining area . . . a separate dining area like this with windows' (personal interview (Jenny), Jenny and Johan, one-bedroom apartment residents). The elegant character of the movement towards the dining area is demonstrated by the fact that the adjoining spaces are functionally subservient: food is prepared in the working part of the kitchen and brought to the dining area, guests

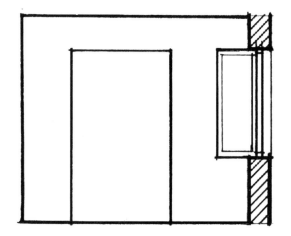

Section of the dining room, view of hallway from the kitchen.

Daylight

The district of Lindholmen occupies a hill overlooking the basin of Sannegård Harbour to one side and the Göta River to the other. The high location and the reflections from the water below give a special character to the light in the neighbourhood and in its apartments:

> I usually say to a lot of the people who come to visit that it's the light. It's a special kind of light, and they've made the most out of it, I think. It's just unbelievable to be greeted by this light every morning, especially in the bay window in the dining area.
>
> (Personal interview, Greta, three-bedroom apartment resident)

The window sashes are subtly moulded, articulating the incoming daylight.

The rooms on the courtyard side are shallow, allowing plenty of daylight to reflect back into the room from the innermost wall surfaces. The effect is most obvious in the dining area, where tall windows extend from wall to wall, washing them with daylight. Partial walls and lintels over openings add to the reflective surface area grazed with light. The shape of the dining area, the size of its windows and the presence of light-reflecting surfaces make it the brightest room in the apartment. These daylighting effects give the room dignity, and make it a stronger goal for movements along the courtyard-side axis. Daylight makes the space important.

The differences in daylight conditions from one room to the next clarify the relative public or private character of each. In the Lindholmen apartment, the street side is not as well lit as the courtyard side. Its darkest room is the bedroom, which is also its most private. The dining area is the most well-lit space in the apartment, and that with the most clearly public character.

Organization of spaces

The deftly resolved relationship between the apartment and its courtyard is a tremendous resource for tenants. Many of my interviews revealed that the Lindholmen courtyard is the scene of a rich social life among residents. The design of the space around the buildings and its relation to the apartments within is an important condition for residents' appropriation of their home environment. From the public streets and spaces in the neighbourhood, the exterior becomes successively more private until we reach the interior of the apartment. The architect described how the older buildings that surround the site provided a source of inspiration:

The dining room's bay window.
View from the courtyard.

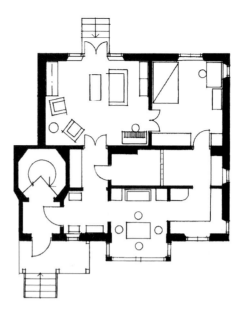

Furnishing schemes from interviews. Scale 1:200.

Territorial boundaries in the courtyard.

1. The great courtyard.
2. The little courtyard space.
3. The front porches.

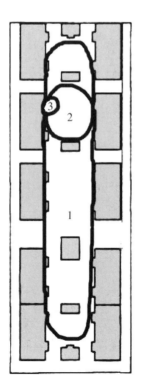

Boundaries allow the relationship between residents and outsiders to be regulated. In the old neighbourhood there were invisible boundaries and territories. We wanted to differentiate the feeling of home from the public realm in various steps, from the larger Lindholmen to your own courtyard and your front porch. There are many small transitions worked into the landscaping until you reach the complete privacy inside your front door. The portal between the street and the courtyard is one such feature, the front porch another.

(Personal interview, Armand Björkman, architect)

The courtyard has three parts with varying degrees of privacy and possession: the great courtyard, the small courtyard spaces and the front porches. The buildings surround a traditional enclosed courtyard. This large oblong space is bounded on the long sides by the apartment buildings, while fences and outbuildings enclose its ends and divide it into two smaller, more private spaces. Even more private are the entrance porches, separated from the small courtyard spaces by fencing, posts and a couple of steps up.

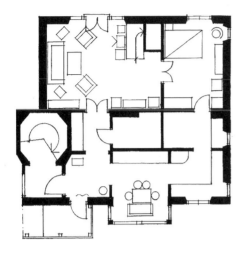 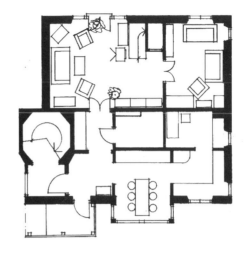

Furnishing schemes from interviews. Scale 1:200.

Some of the residents consider the smaller courtyard spaces as bounded by two buildings, some by four buildings. The perceived size depends on the way in which they socialize with their neighbours. The human scale of the development, the short distance across the courtyard, means that everyone knows who lives in which building. According to Jenny:

> The distance across is just right – you can't see in entirely, but you can tell who it is when someone comes out. It's just right to say hello to someone on the other side.
>
> (Personal interview (Jenny), Jenny and Johan, one-bedroom apartment residents)

Greta's impression was the same, even though her apartment is one floor up from the level of the courtyard. She told me:

> You see people here all the time, and if an outsider comes . . . of course I know who lives in these four buildings.
>
> (Personal interview, Greta, three-bedroom apartment resident)

Front porch.

Arbetaregatan. Photo: Charles Hörnstein.

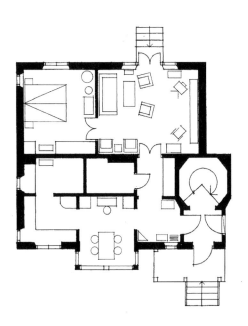

The little courtyard space.

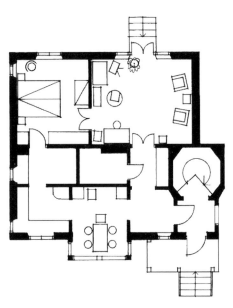

Furnishing schemes from interviews.
Scale 1:200.

Residents' sense of territoriality extends beyond the small courtyard space to the whole block, the entire development, and the surrounding district. Elsa described her and Erik's view of their neighbourhood:

> We feel at home . . . when we turn down Miragatan, where you're just taken aback by Lindholmen, I think, yes, that's for sure, that's when you feel like you're home.
>
> (Personal interview (Elsa), Elsa and Erik, one-bedroom apartment residents)

The oblong courtyard is separated from Verkmästaregatan and Plåtslagaregatan by portals, and from Lindholmsvägen, Arbetaregatan and Släggaregatan by openings between buildings. The boundaries between the courtyard and the surrounding neighbourhood are clear. Frida described for me how and when she feels like she has arrived at home:

> I guess it's when you come from the street outside and turn into the courtyard. Then again, sometimes you take the bus, and then it's when you come over the crown of Bonnabacken hill and you see your own house.
>
> (Personal interview, Frida, three-bedroom apartment resident)

The portals are clear boundaries between different degrees of privacy and different territories. They signal that the courtyard space is entirely different from the space of the street. The courtyard belongs to the residents without excluding outsiders or visitors. On the contrary, the clarity of the boundary alleviates any tension between residents and visitors by making it clear who controls the space.

> There's a real sense of inside and outside here. A whole busload of people can come out just to look around the area. But this courtyard – no one comes in here without some reason.
>
> (Personal interview (Jenny), Jenny and Johan, one-bedroom apartment residents)

All tenants of this development are members of a housing co-operative that takes responsibility for the maintenance of the courtyard. The co-op adds legitimacy to residents' territoriality by making it clear that they have the right to control the courtyard. They plant flowers there, maintain planters and green lawns, and so forth. With this work they mark the territory they control. Elsa and her husband are among those who

Entrance to the courtyard from Verkmästaregatan street.

actively participate in adorning the courtyard with flowers. Elsa told me,

> It's clear that the courtyard is ours, that's for sure. But people walking by are welcome to come in and have a look at our flowers.
>> (Personal interview (Elsa), Elsa and Erik, one-bedroom apartment residents)

The division of the courtyard into smaller spaces gives residents a chance to establish territory in successive stages. Johan told of how his and Jenny's territory has developed:

> It has changed. At first is was just here, the area next to the front porch, but now it's much wider, extending throughout the whole area.
>> (Personal interview (Johan), Johan and Jenny, one-bedroom apartment residents)

The dining area provides an important point of contact between the exterior space of the courtyard and the interior space of the home. From here residents can discover, analyse and make recognizable the boundaries and territories of the courtyard. The openness of the dining area orients the apartment and its residents towards the courtyard. In the dining area they can see and be seen, which gives them the feeling that they can monitor the whole of their building and its courtyard. With its bay window, the dining area symbolically penetrates the outside wall, entering the room outside. The architects' use of daylight, movement, axiality and enclosing details accentuates this penetration but at the same time provides enough spatial security to allow the residents to watch over the courtyard. The dining area is a border space between inside and out, and an important component of the process of appropriation.

Greta's comments show how residents monitor events in the courtyard. The clear boundaries help resi-

The little courtyard space is bordered by two opposing houses and transverse courtyard buildings.

dents to understand these events, identify where the boundaries lie and recognize who is moving in what territory:

> I don't know exactly, but it's just as if these four [buildings surrounding one of the smaller courtyard spaces] kind of belong together – we just see more of one another.
>
> (Personal interview, Greta, three-bedroom apartment resident)

The courtyard's intimate dimensions facilitate visual communication between the apartments and the courtyard and from one apartment to another. For Frida, control over the courtyard is an integral part of her life at home:

> I really want to know if [my neighbours] are at home – I've become like that. I used to be more anonymous, but since I moved in here I think it's fun. It's kind of a Japanese thing – to see without seeing – noticing when they come home, and so on.
>
> (Personal interview, Frida, three-bedroom apartment resident)

The dining area's proximity to the entrance makes it naturally the most public space in the apartment. The living room has a more private atmosphere. The dining area can be furnished in a variety of ways, and there's enough room for play and other activities. Its primary function is as a space for daily meals, but this is also where residents gather on many other occasions – reading the paper after work, doing homework, children's play and receiving guests. All of my interviews were conducted in the dining area, for example. Frida told me:

> You can have a dining table in the living room if you want, of course, but as far as we're concerned we want to sit right here. You've got kids running in and out, sitting here and eating, and small children lying on the floor, and neighbours coming in – somehow everything happens here.
>
> (Personal interview, Frida, three-bedroom apartment resident)

The fact that the dining area is in the midst of a variety of activities, yet not burdened by their daily routine, reinforces its spatial dignity. Architect Armand Björkman explained the value of delineating the kitchen from the dining area, saying that 'Separating the kitchen was another way of emphasizing the importance of the dining area'.

Case study Stumholmen

Description

Case study Stumholmen examines three identical two-bedroom apartments of 82m² (883 sq ft), completed in 1993. The apartments were designed by Kjell Forshed of Brunnberg & Forshed Arkitektkontor.

Stumholmen is an island just east of the heart of the town of Karlskrona. The Swedish navy owned the island until 1991, using it to warehouse equipment and provisions. Stumholmen had a bakery, butchers, clothing factory and a variety of different warehouses. The National Federation of Tenants' Savings and Building Societies (HSB) bought the island in 1991, and the following year initiated a programme of renovation and new construction for the 1993 housing expo, Bo93.

Västra Kungshall, gable to the west.

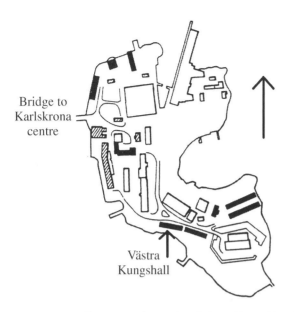

Bridge to
Karlskrona
centre

Västra
Kungshall

The arrow points to Stumholmen, Västra Kungshall.

(8.5ft). Two stairwells accessible from the land side serve four apartments each, two per floor.

The Stumholmen apartment is composed of six rough squares of 12 to 14m² (129–151 sq ft), two of which are divided into two small rooms. Three of the six have dedicated functions: bathroom/storage and kitchen towards the street, entrance/loggia towards the sea. The loggia is an inset balcony – a consequence of a strict masterplan that forbids projecting balconies out of consideration for the existing buildings. The other three squares are flexible-use rooms.

The organization of spaces differs from that of the standard Functionalist apartment in several important details: one can walk a circuit through its rooms, some of the rooms are accessible only from other living spaces, and some are not functionally determinate. This organization has similarities to earlier housing types (in Sweden) such as the six-room 'double-row house'.

The case study apartments are within a new building called Västra Kungshall, which was constructed for the expo. The long and narrow two-storey building includes eight units. Its interior width is less than 8m (26ft), and the ceiling height throughout is 2.6m

We talked a lot about 3.6m [12ft] modules, and that's about how it turned out. This idea of the unit room has been around for a long time, as well as the possibilities offered by a long and narrow building. You see it in so many great old timbered buildings.

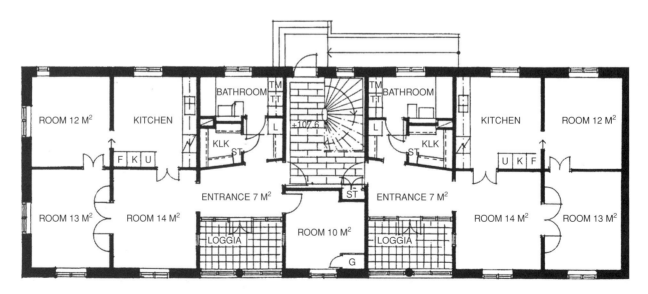

[*this page and facing page*] Floor plan. Scale 1:200.

Every single parsonage in the country looks essentially that way.

(Personal interview, Kjell Forshed, architect)

Residents have the liberty of deciding for themselves how to use three of the rooms. The six-square organization of the plan means they can have two living rooms and a single bedroom, or one of the living rooms can be a walk-through space while the other is used as a second bedroom. The generality of the spaces and the flexibility of the layout create the conditions in which residents can individually interpret their own living situation.

I first visited the Stumholmen apartment during the Bo93 housing expo. I was strongly impressed by the use of beautiful materials, treatment of daylight, the openness of the loggia and the unusual organization of spaces. I undertook the case study of the apartment during the spring and summer of 1995. Early on it was clear that *axiality* would play an important role. Other attributes that emerged during analysis of the apartment were *spatial figure*, *daylight* and *materials and detailing*. I was greatly aided by fictional texts in formulating my impressions of the place, particularly the effect of materials and details on my perception.

The rooms have contrasting expressions making it easier to identify and describe the various attributes. In my attempts to describe what gives these rooms their architectural character, Dom Hans van der Laan's theories of space were a source of inspiration and substantial support.[1] These helped me define the important relationships between wall and opening, surface and mass, and interior and exterior space. The *enclosure* field of attributes took form.

The Stumholmen apartment is characterized by a clear contrast in illuminance from one room to another. Many of the comments from residents centred on the marvellous light in the apartment and the beauty of its windows. Anders succeeded in capturing the ineffable character of this light:

It's a part of that summer feeling. When the sun is beating down and reflecting off the water, there's a particularly pleasing light throughout the apartment – I don't know how to describe it.

(Personal interview, Anders, two-bedroom apartment resident)

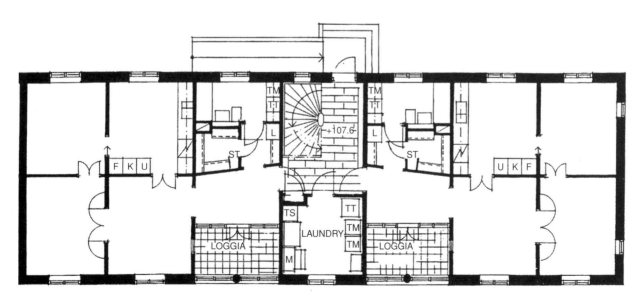

The treatment of daylight and detailing of the windows were also prominent in my interview with the apartment's architect, Kjell Forshed. Describing the light in the Stumholmen apartment generated the field of attributes I call *daylight*.

Materials and detailing

There is an atmosphere in the Stumholmen apartment that is often associated with old country houses. This atmosphere has nothing to do with nostalgia; it is largely based on the strong impression made by the use of materials and the feeling we get in the presence of something authentic. Materials and details express care for a building's occupants in many ways. For the architect, the choice of materials was an important part of the project. The pine floorboards have been steeped in lye in the traditional manner to lighten them.

Loggia, view from hallway.
Photo: Jappe Liljedahl.

> The most important thing is the wood floor. A pine floor creates a feeling of beautiful simplicity. It's the flooring material of the eighteenth century, when poverty dominated Swedish housing. It's part of ordinary farm and country culture. It's a much more austere floor. You can compare ours to the new house next door, designed by Myhrenbergs architects – their floors are wood, too. They used oak, which also looks good, but has a more affluent feeling. It's harder and it echoes a little more.
>
> (Personal interview, Kjell Forshed)

The outside walls are made of aerated concrete blocks 40cm (16in) thick, rendered outside in yellow and red, and wallpapered inside. The ceilings have rosettes in their centres, complete with outlets for light fixtures, and are painted white. The skirting and door trim have mitred corners and were painted grey on site. The juncture between the skirting and the moulded architrave that surrounds the door openings is resolved with a plinth block.

The windows are pressed to the outside plane of the walls, which gives deep window niches with splayed sides. Radiators are set into these niches below the windows. Window frames and sashes are richly moulded.

The loggia is delineated by a floor-to-ceiling window wall with four venting sashes. The hall has a corresponding glazed French door. The floor of the loggia is paved with blue tiles. A small round window is set into the wall between the loggia and the living room.

From the interviews it is clear that residents have a close relationship with the materials and details of their homes. They sense in the details that someone has made a conscientious effort on their behalf, commenting appreciatively on the wood floors, the tile in the loggia, and the round window.

They are met by well-executed craftsmanship in the treatment of the floor, the mitred trim and the onsite painting of the woodwork. These apartments also have many unusual details such as the ceiling rosettes, French doors, window wall and window niches. There are materials here that we experience as authentic. Calle's description of the wood floor illustrates this point:

Detailing; floor meets wall and door opening.
Photo: Jappe Liljedahl.

Ceiling with rosette. Photo: Sten Gromark.

Yes, I've thought about it – it's something I care about – that we don't have a bunch of plastic here. I think that's so nice. It's one of those feelings that's part of what makes it good and cozy. I just wish more apartments looked like this. And it's just wonderful when you wash these floors, scrub them with soft soap.

(Personal interview, Calle, two-bedroom apartment resident)

Axiality

Axial paths and lines of sight are of great importance to one's experience of the Stumholmen apartment. The primary longitudinal axis is slightly canted, and there are two secondary transverse axes and a secondary longitudinal axis. This system of axes is complemented by a powerful gesture from the hall towards the sea through the loggia's inside and outside layers of glazing. Axiality has an important influence over our movement in this apartment, and establishes an atmosphere in which we feel free to move from room to room.

The rooms are interconnected by paths and sight-lines. From each room we can observe the lighting conditions and atmosphere in one or more of the other rooms. Axiality makes the apartment 'surveyable';

it is presented to the visitor from the entrance by the primary longitudinal axis. Calle described his impressions of entering the apartment:

I think it's amazing. The thing is that you don't just have the usual square when you come in through the door – that appeals to me. Something happens immediately, with the angled wall of the hallway and then the outdoor room.

(Personal interview, Calle, two-bedroom apartment resident)

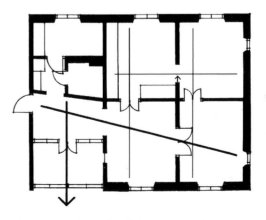

The apartment's axiality. Primary axes and secondary axes. Scale 1:200.

Chain of rooms towards the sea. View from hallway.
Photo from show apartment at the Bo 93 expo.
Photo: Jappe Liljedahl.

The longitudinal axis has been created by interconnecting a row of three adjoining rooms through aligned openings –a wide flat archway and a pair of large French doors. The architect seizes the opportunity to create the longest possible axis, crossing the length of the apartment through these rooms. This orders the place about a clear axial direction.

This primary axis extends from its obvious point of departure in the entrance hall to the far living room. From the hall we can read the invitation to move diagonally through the middle living room, then through French doors to the far living room.

It's a real addition to the apartment – a movement that we accentuated with the placement of rugs in the model unit at Bo93. We placed the door openings so that they 'drift' diagonally.

(Personal interview, Kjell Forshed, architect)

Moving along the main axis confirms what we observe in our initial survey from the starting point in the hall. Details such as the influx of daylight and the dignity of the spaces encourage this movement. In the end units the effect is augmented by a window in the gable wall.

The two secondary axes extend from the window on the north facade to those on the south facade, penetrating the spine wall through narrow door openings. The longitudinal axis crosses the transverse axes at two points in the living rooms. The other rooms and the principal views are revealed from these points. These axial crossings are therefore important architectural elements that heighten the intensity of our experience. The hallway is another important point at which the primary axis meets the gesture towards the sea.

The apartment's axes play a significant role in the integration of interior and exterior space. Axiality accentuates the apartment's most visually important features, thereby supporting the process of appropriation by residents.

A final longitudinal axis connects the two main street-side rooms with each other. In the Stumholmen apartment we find a clear differentiation between the primary and secondary axes. The main axis is given greater dignity by its broad openings, its length and the greater number of rooms it connects, and the similarities in form, material and expression of those rooms. By contrast, the secondary axes are shorter and cross fewer rooms through narrower openings.

Enclosure

An important part of the character of the Stumholmen apartment is the clear contrast between open and closed spaces. The openness of the hall and loggia is offset by the enclosure of the living rooms, kitchen and bedroom. Anders indicated how the wide doorways allow residents to vary the degree of enclosure:

> I don't like having a bunch of closed doors; it's got to be as open as possible and make a breezy impression.
>
> (Personal interview, Anders, two-bedroom apartment resident)

The shape and placement of openings are important conditions for the sense of enclosure. In the living rooms, the shape and placement of the windows and doors hold our attention within the boundaries of the room despite their relatively large size. Thresholds and glazing bars help us to visually interpret the sections of wall that have been removed. The doorways have headers over them and the white paint of the ceiling has been stretched down over the top of the wall, making the rooms more distinct. Clearly articulated corners accentuate the quality of enclosure. The enclosed character of the rooms makes the treatment of

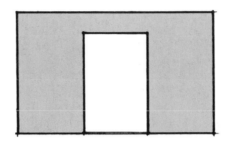

Wall between the living rooms. The shape of the wall surface dominates over the opening.

materials and finishing details more prominent, as the architect pointed out:

> We had to fight for the thresholds. We wanted them because the rooms are supposed to be clearly defined to allow the materials to meet.
>
> (Personal interview, Kjell Forshed, architect)

The sense of enclosure is emphasized by the symmetrical placement of windows. The shape of the wall surface dominates that of its openings. The composition of outside walls is similar to that of the transverse partitions. In the living rooms, the windows and broad French doors are centred on their walls, giving the rooms visual balance.

> The windows were important, and setting them in the middle of the wall makes them good rooms. We wanted tranquil spaces, balanced spaces. I have an aversion to windows placed right up against adjoining walls. People put furniture in front of the windows anyway, and they're so well made now that you don't get a cold downdraft next to them anymore. We can get rid of the old rules and place a window precisely, beautifully, right in the centre, and put the sofa in front of it.
>
> (Personal interview, Kjell Forshed, architect)

The splayed sides of the window niches underscore the thickness and therefore the mass of the walls. Interior and exterior space meet through distinctly

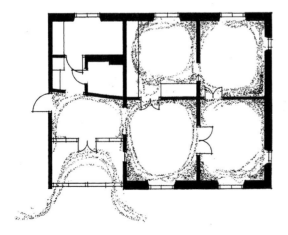

The apartment's enclosure, marked in heavy lines. Scale 1:200.

Enclosure, distinct corners, symmetrically placed openings, marked spatial contours, deep window niches. Photo from show apartment at the Bo 93 expo. Photo: Jappe Liljedahl.

designed openings. The design of the windows in the Stumholmen apartment gives a visual manifestation of the mass of the surrounding walls. The openings show and elucidate the implications of the boundary between inside and out. The divided-light windows set in thick masonry walls create a feeling of security inside in relation to the unknown space beyond. The glazing bars diminish the effect of opening the walls, and the splayed embrasures accentuate the protective capacity of the surrounding walls.

The apartment's open spaces – the hall and the loggia – face outward towards the sea, the view drawing our attention away from the interior of the room. The divided-light window walls that separate the hall from the loggia and the loggia from the world outside open the rooms, allowing them to overlap. The glazing layers divide the rooms only physically: spatially the hall, loggia and exterior are integrated. The hall and the

loggia bring the outside world into the apartment at the same time revealing the interior to the world.

Movement

The Stumholmen apartment offers possibilities for several types of movement. This flexibility is very important to residents' perception and use of the apartment. They can walk a circular loop from room to room around the spine wall. There are movements along the axes with rhythms that depend upon the size, shape and lighting conditions of the rooms they cross. The architect even utilizes the element of surprise where we emerge from the dim stairwell to find the brightly lit loggia beckoning.

The circular path replaces the radial circulation pattern typical of the Functionalist apartment in which all rooms are accessible from a neutral hall. This circuit offers greater flexibility as rooms can be reached from more than one direction. It combines the various axial paths and sightlines, enriching our experience of the apartment.

Anders had chosen to seal the passage between kitchen and bedroom, turning the bedroom from a walk-through to a dead-end room. This has made the apartment's innermost space into a clearly private realm:

And I like the fact that the bedroom is a little separated from the rest of the apartment. I don't want

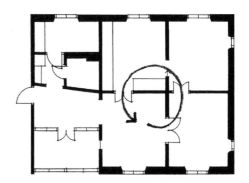

Circulation loop. Scale 1:200.

to rush right into the kitchen from the bedroom. So I asked to have it sealed and we worked it out. It's no great inconvenience to go around like this.

(Personal interview, Anders, two-bedroom apartment resident)

Part of the appeal of the apartment's circular organization is that residents can choose to close off an opening between two rooms, either by sealing a wall as Anders did or simply by closing a door.

In the Stumholmen apartment, the rooms circle around the central spine wall. We move from one of the larger living spaces to another without having to pass through a smaller intermediate space such as a hall. The similarity of the rooms gives the movement through the apartment an even tempo.

The bright light of the loggia is in contrast to the dimly lit stairwell, part of a sequence orchestrated by the architect:

People wondered why our stairwells were so dark. They thought we should have put the stairs on the sea side. But we wanted to hold back with the view instead of giving it all away before you even get into the apartment. First you enter a murky space where you're kind of kept on a leash a little, and then it comes.

(Personal interview, Kjell Forshed, architect)

The sequence has three steps:

1) *Anticipation* is established outside, at the front door. The space here is vast, boundless, filled with daylight. The front door is set into a stone-clad niche that calls attention to the opportunity to make an entrance, to pass through the wall.
2) The anticipation *accumulates* in the spatially closed stairwell. Two small windows introduce a little muted daylight. The stairwell is an intermediate space – a space between inside and out. Standing here we see the doors that lead into the interiors of the various apartments. There is one more border to cross.
3) *Surprise* is the goal of the sequence – the surprise of coming into a brightly lit hall that introduces the private realm of the home. The contrast to the darkness and enclosure of the stairwell is strong and clear. The influx of light and the magnificent view of the sea make for a powerful experience. The movement from dark to light, closed to open, concludes with a surprise.

The element of surprise that Froshed has incorporated within the pattern of movement at Stumholmen is important to our subconscious perception of architecture. Strong contrasts and the combination of anticipation and fulfilment make for a striking architectural experience.

Chain of rooms. Photo from show apartment at the Bo 93 expo. Photo: Jappe Liljedahl.

Choreographed movement
in three steps. Anticipation.

Surprise, loggia.
Photo: Sten Gromark

Spatial figure

The floor plan of the Stumholmen apartment is rectangular. It is divided longitudinally into two areas of equal depth by a central spine wall. The spatial figures of these rooms differ from those of the standard Functionalist apartment. They are set into six similar squares each of about 12 to 14m² (129–150 sq ft). Two are divided into smaller rooms, a third holds the kitchen, and the three remaining squares form the large rooms of the apartment. The hall and loggia are medium-sized spaces of about 7m² (75 sq ft) each. The rest of the rooms are small, between 2 and 5m² (22 and 54 sq ft): a walk-in wardrobe, a cloakroom and a bathroom.

I've been wanting to do that for a long time – make a room that is at rest, more or less square. We talked a lot about 3.6m [12ft] modules ... This idea of

View of living room from the kitchen.

the unit room has been around a long time, as well as the possibilities offered by a long and narrow building . . . I wanted to make rooms with beautiful proportions.

(Personal interview, Kjell Forshed, architect)

The ceiling height, slightly more than standard at 2.6m (8.5ft), in combination with the length and width dimensions, gives the rooms more cubic proportions than are common in residential spaces.

Daylight

The development of construction standards and code regulations was influenced by an increasingly rational view of daylight conditions in the home. At the Bo93 housing expo in Karlskrona, Stumholmen, great effort was demonstrated in exploring the non-measurable qualities of the window. A group of architects and window manufacturers presented a window they had designed paying particular attention to residents' perception of incoming daylight. Both frame and sash of the new window were moulded. Panes of two-layer insulated glass with a low-emissivity film replaced their heavy three-layer predecessors, allowing for more slender construction.

Daylight is an important element in the experience of the Stumholmen apartment, due in part to the difference in illuminance from one room to another,

but also in the detailing of the openings in the facade. The rooms are shallow and the windows tall, allowing the spine wall to be directly illuminated by sunlight. The spine wall reflects this light back into the rooms. The light-coloured floor also reflects daylight, and a great deal of reflected light gathers at the centre of each room. Britta and Bertil gave their impressions of the light in their apartment:

The view we have here is not exactly the same every day. The light shifts – it's a special kind of sea light that changes from day to day. There's always a new atmosphere. Somehow there's a different kind of light over the whole island. The light inside the apartment is unusual. At first I didn't think there was

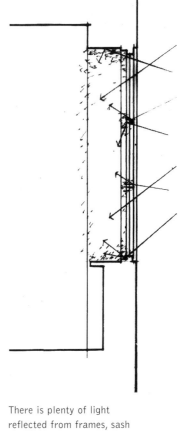

There is plenty of light reflected from frames, sash and splayed sides in the window niche.

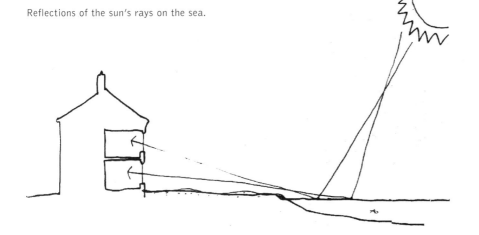

Reflections of the sun's rays on the sea.

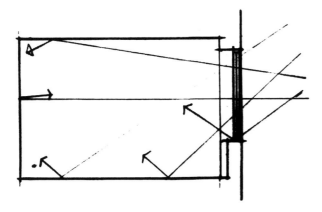

The daylight reflected from the sea strikes the south side of the building parallel and even below.

Window detail.
Photo: Jappe Liljedahl.

anything special about the windows, but it happened more and more. It's also because you can see through from one side to the other.

(Personal interview, Britta and Bertil, two-bedroom apartment residents)

The rooms facing the sea are brighter than those on the street side. Much of the character of the light in the apartment is formed by events outside the building. The influx of direct sunlight is complemented by reflections of the sun's rays in the waves of the sea. This reflected light strikes the south side of the building from below – an unusual effect. As a result, even the ceilings serve as reflectors of direct light. The rooms seem to be lit from above and to be washed with an unusual amount of light.

The illuminance of the rooms is graded. All the residents interviewed use the innermost room as a bedroom; this is the apartment's darkest room. The level of illuminance increases thereafter from the kitchen to the living rooms, hall, and finally to the loggia, the apartment's most public and brightest room.

The windows open outward. Together with the slender dimensions of the sashes, this allows the frames and mullions to be thoroughly washed in daylight. Photo: Jappe Liljedahl

The placement of the windows flush with the outside surface of the wall makes for deep window niches inside. The splayed sides are painted white to reflect daylight deep into the room and to maximize the perceived size of the openings.

The casement windows open outward. Together with the slender dimensions of the sashes this allows the frames and mullions to be thoroughly washed in daylight. Frame and sash are both moulded and painted in a matt green-grey tone. The matt paint broadens and evens out reflections. The rich play of light and shadow over the windows' rounded mouldings articulates the border between interior and exterior space.

The window niches are filled with light reflected from the frames, sashes and canted sides. Daylight penetrates into the apartment from outside through the intermediate space of the niche. Here, diffuse light reflected from various sources mixes with sharper direct light to produce a condensed, intense light. Light bounces between the sides of the niche. The direct influx of light falls heavy and thick into the room, coloured and filled out by its passage through the niche. The play of light in the window and its niche moderates the glare effect, as is indirectly demonstrated by the following story from Calle:

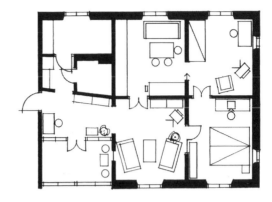

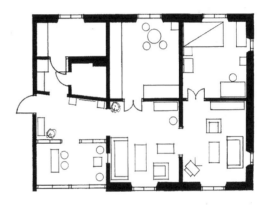

Furnishing schemes 1 (upper), 2, from interviews with residents. Scale 1:200.

> I remember when Kjell Forshed was here. Of course we had to put up curtains. We used the ones we already had – there was nothing wrong with them. But Kjell said that these windows aren't made for curtains. We tore them down the instant he left. It's terrific, you know – we don't need curtains!
>
> (Personal interview, Calle, two-bedroom apartment resident)

Organization of spaces

The Stumholmen apartment can be rearranged in a number of different ways. The residents place great value on the opportunity to decide for themselves the use of each room and the organization of the whole. There is no designated function for each space, and

there are various ways of dividing the apartment into private and public zones.

- In *Furnishing Scheme 1*, two bedrooms make up the most private and intimate part of the apartment. The kitchen is somewhat more isolated than the most public area, which is made up of the living room, hall and loggia.

- In *Furnishing Scheme 2*, the passage between kitchen and bedroom has been sealed. The single bedroom thereby becomes decidedly the most private room in the home. The inner living room is for watching television; it is furnished primarily for the residents rather than for company. Visitors are received in the outer living room, and invited out to the loggia.

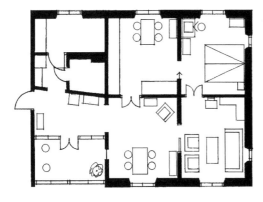

Furnishing scheme 3, from interviews with residents.
Scale 1:200.

In this scheme the kitchen is a workplace, not for socializing, and is more private than the hall, loggia and living rooms.

- In *Furnishing Scheme 3*, the side facing the sea is the public area of the apartment. The bedroom and kitchen are more private.

Britta speculated about how the content of the various rooms could evolve:

Loggia. Photo of show apartment at the Bo 93 expo.
Photo: Jappe Liljedahl.

I often think about what would happen if I got old and very sick and bedridden. Then I imagine re-arranging everything and putting the bed in the inner living room so that I could lie there and look out at the sea.

(Personal interview (Britta), Britta and Bertil, two-bedroom apartment residents)

The freedom to rearrange the apartment demonstrated above is built on the attributes discussed in the preceding chapters. The hall and three largest spaces share the same materials and detailing, giving them equal dignity. None of the rooms is degraded to the status of bedroom or elevated to the status of living room by virtue of its materials or form. The degree of enclosure and the proportions of these rooms are equal. The function of each room is left to the residents' individual taste; the content and meaning of each is not actually determined until it is put to use. The organization of the apartment makes this flexibility possible. The radial circulation pattern of the standard Functionalist apartment, in which each room is entered only from a neutral hallway, is replaced here by axially aligned sequences of walk-through rooms. Together, the detailing, shape and organization of the spaces allow residents to establish zones for different activities, atmospheres and degrees of privacy.

The island of Stumholmen is used by the residents for walks and neighbourhood socializing. It has a strong neighbourhood identity in the community of Karls-krona, separated by a clear boundary from adjoining districts. Calle described the sense of community on the island:

We've got quite a few acquaintances here on the island. Several people from where I work and from the local government live here.

(Personal interview, Calle, two-bedroom apartment resident)

History is a tangible part of this residential environment. Memories of the island's former use for producing and storing naval provisions in simple warehouse structures have been kept alive by the sensitive renovation of existing buildings and the adaptation of new construction to local traditions.

According to the masterplan, Stumholmen's main use is recreation. All land on the island is, and shall remain, accessible to the public. As a result the outside of the building is also a boundary for residents' possession of the space around their homes. The outer plane of the wall thus forms the legal and perceptual border between public and private. From the loggia, tenants can sit inside this border, within the private sphere of the home, and observe what happens outside without playing an active role in it.

The water that surrounds the Stumholmen apartment is the kind of landscape that symbolizes freedom and infinity. The sea is also strongly tied to Karlskrona's identity as a military city. The loggia's window wall is a point of contact between the home and the sea:

According to the masterplan, Stumholmen's main use is recreation. All land on the island is and shall remain accessible to the public. As a result, the outside of the building is also a boundary for residents' possession of the space around their homes. The outer place of the wall thus forms the legal and perceptual border between public and private.

> Well they call it a balcony but it's actually a room in the apartment. However it feels like it's outside when I open these four windows, because then I can hear the sea, I hear the birds, the sun glitters on the water, you can feel the wind in here. It gives it a different feeling.
>
> (Personal interview, Anders, two-bedroom apartment resident)

The loggia's function as a border space is to negotiate a bond between the seascape and the home. The apartment opens to the world outside through the hall and the loggia. The loggia is critical in anchoring the building and each of its apartments to the site. In the summer, residents move furniture out to the loggia, to the other side of its protective glass shell. Ground-floor residents climb over a bottom row of fixed glass to get to the public property outside. Awkward, perhaps, as Britta acknowledges,

> But we are aware of it – that Stumholmen is supposed to be accessible to everyone. If we had doors here and could walk right out, then we would just keep expanding more and more, I know we would. When we open up here in the summer, open all four windows, well it's not the same as sitting out on a deck outside your own home, it's not the same, but still it's something in between. At first I missed the feeling of being able to walk right out. That was a limitation. We have quite a few close friends, and we know a lot of people out here. Now they can come right up and look in on us, but we get to decide if we say, 'Come on in'.
>
> (Personal interview (Britta), Britta and Bertil, two-bedroom apartment residents)

To a visitor, the lack of a delineated private outdoor room seems confining, a limitation in the home environment. However, none of the residents interviewed saw this as a disadvantage. Some of them were explicitly positive, like Bertil, who pointed out that 'you don't have to be bothered with breaking your back in the garden'. The ability of residents to determine the pace of their social lives and the extent of their responsibilities around the home is in this case an advantage. Not to have to participate is a positive aspect of apartment living, as Britta's comments illustrate:[7]

> So I guess we think it's pretty nice that we're the ones who decide when we're social. If you get too friendly with the neighbours, there's a risk that you stop living your own life.
> (Personal interview (Britta), Britta and Bertil, two-bedroom apartment residents)

Contact between the apartment and its surroundings is primarily visual. Along the water's edge, south of the building, is a pathway that is heavily used during the summer. Sometimes public accessibility to the grounds around the building is perceived as bothersome:

> Sure, some days during the summer there's a tremendous amount of traffic out there; just so long as they don't come up and put their hands to the windows and look in.
> (Personal interview, Britta and Bertil, two-bedroom apartment residents)

The boundary between the private sphere of the home and the public realm outside is unclear. The fact that strangers may come up and look through the windows is a sign that the territorial boundaries surrounding the home are not working satisfactorily. Nothing outside the building clearly demonstrates that the grounds belong to either the residents or the public. The city plan leaves no room for clarifying the matter of possession with border zones or other territorial markings.

Case study Hestra

Description
Case study Hestra comprises five one- to four-bedroom apartments in the Nielsen block of the Hestra housing development in Borås. They were built in 1992–3 after drawings by Jens Thomas Arnfred of the Danish architectural firm Vandkunstens Tegnestue.

The district lies on the west edge of town. The hilly landscape is covered by a dark and thick coniferous wood interspersed here and there with meadows, hillocks and patches of deciduous forest. Old roads and stone fences bear witness to a bygone era of small-scale farming. The Nielsen block is made up of 10 buildings with a total of 44 apartments. The buildings are long and narrow and radiate out into the landscape from two oak-covered hilltops, four buildings ringing the hill to the south and six to the north.

Each building emerges horizontally from the hill, and as the grade drops away the building height grows from one to three stories. A driveable walkway winds around the hill, passing through a large portal in each building, linking them together. Between buildings are open courtyards from which the apartments can be entered. A couple of these also have a few parking places. The buildings are clad in corrugated black fibre-reinforced cement sheeting. Architect Jens Arnfred revealed his inspiration for the scheme:

> Sometimes you surprise yourself, you know – where does the inspiration come from? But one thing I can tell you: over there north of the buildings lies an old house, a farm. There's a barn there, and I think this is actually a common Swedish principle, that you can drive in with hay up here, on the upper level, and I think they've probably got cows down below, and it's red-stained wood. That was the first thing I saw when I came here, and I thought, that's so exciting! That is in fact where the inspiration for these buildings comes from. But inspiration is nothing you study – it's usually something just around the corner, and often part of the Nordic building tradition.
> (Personal interview, Jens Arnfred, architect)

The two long facades of each building have different functions – entrances on one side, outdoor rooms on

The Nielsen block of the Hestra housing development.
The southern group of buildings.

 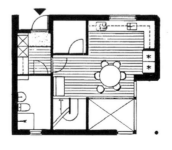 

Gable apartment with three floors, four bedrooms.
Illustration Vandkunsten.
Scale 1:200

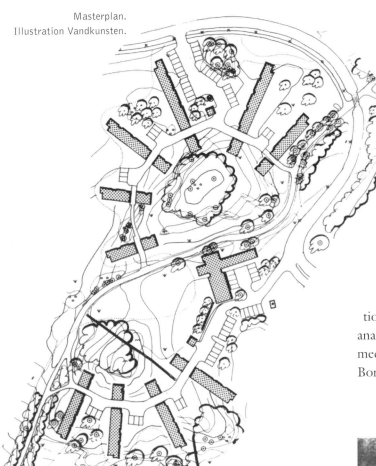

Masterplan.
Illustration Vandkunsten.

I conducted the case study research at Hestra during the spring of 1996. As this work progressed I gained an insight into how much the residents valued the architect's interpretation of the site. Many of them described the importance to them of integration of the buildings with the site. Architect Jens Arnfred, too, went to great trouble to describe his work in siting the buildings and moulding them after the natural features of the site. Case study Hestra helped me develop the concepts of *place*, *territory* and *appropriation* with support from the writings of Christian Norberg-Schulz.

I tried to develop my understanding of the relationship between building and site by describing and analysing the *border space* of the home – the space that mediates between the home and the natural landscape. Border space is a result of the interpretation of the site,

Perspective of the southern group of buildings.
From the Borås 94 expo catalogue.

the other. The entrance doors are set into niches in the facade. Rather than sharing common stairwells, all of the apartments have direct entrances from the yard. The outdoor rooms are either balconies or wood-framed decks, depending on the gradient at that point.

I first visited the Hestra apartments during the Nordisk bostadsmässa '94 housing expo. I was strongly impressed by the openness of the apartments from one floor to another and towards the landscape outside, by the spatial dynamics of the scheme, and by the use of daylight. I also appreciated the sensitive treatment of the surrounding natural landscape.

and helps anchor the building to it. In this case study the *enclosure* and *daylight* fields of attributes were important to the perception of the home.

Materials and detailing

Materials and detailing are in the foreground of my impression of the Hestra apartments. The architect told an interviewer: 'We have avoided using artificial material wherever it was possible'.[2]

The textured black cladding of the exterior is contrasted by smooth white gypsum-board walls inside. The flooring throughout is varnished beech hardwood. The bathroom walls are clad in white tile, with the ceiling and top of the walls painted blue. The interior

Yards to the two- and three-bedroom apartments.

Gable. Photo: Sten Gromark.

trim is stained a rust colour and the white walls frame two-storey window openings. A ribbon window runs under the eaves around the entire building, making the broad overhangs visible from inside. The top floor has cathedral ceilings, and on the gable ends the tops of the windows follow the pitch of the roof. A characteristic detail is the vertical opening between floors that ties the dining area to the living room to form a large common space.

Hestra residents demonstrated in my interviews with them an unusually conscious relationship to the materials and details of their apartments. The sloped gable windows, cathedral ceiling, window walls and opening between floor levels are some of the unusual details the residents interpreted as signs that care had been taken on their behalf. Karin told me:

I think the trim around the doors is so cool. These natural materials, they stand out – it's the same thing with the hardwood floors – much more when everything around them is neutral. You never get tired of the white walls. Now loud wallpaper you get tired of. And then if you've got a lot of great art and things like that they stand out much more.

(Personal interview, Karin, four-bedroom apartment resident)

Niklas was more pragmatic in his praise for the white-painted gypsum-board walls, calling them 'perfect, superior. If they get dirty you just use a little bleach, or roll on a little paint' (personal interview (Niklas), Niklas and Lena, four-bedroom apartment residents).

The wood floors and white interior walls make a harmonious impression. The detailing is fairly rough: there is no moulded trim or delicate woodwork. The white walls stand in defiant contrast to the natural landscape outside. The materials in the Hestra apartments do not have the substance or craftsmanship seen at Stumholmen.

The white walls are also perceived as an expression of wilful simplicity and symbolize for some of the residents a way of living. Olle described the atmosphere as 'Nothing extra, just totally functional. That appealed to both of us. We liked the strict, no-frills approach'

Floor opening. Living room on ground-floor, four-bedroom apartment.

Kitchen and dining area, two-bedroom apartment.
Photo: Ulf Nilsson.

(personal interview (Olle), Olle and Petra, three-bedroom apartment residents).

The residents' appreciation for this simplicity is connected to the feeling that something that feels real and right is authentic. The materials and detailing at Hestra demonstrate a consideration for the inhabitants that has nothing to do with exclusive finishes; care can just as well be conveyed by the unusual or eccentric, or by questioning standard, traditional practices. In describing the impression made on her by the white walls, Nina told me:

When the whole place is white . . . somehow it's like somebody has told you that it's not the walls themselves that are important, but rather what you put on them.

(Personal interview, Nina, two-bedroom apartment resident)

The materials and detailing of the apartments can in many ways initiate the process of appropriation by the residents.

Axiality

Axiality plays an understated role in the perception of these apartments. The various rooms are entered from neutral spaces.

An opening between floors forms a vertical direction, a kind of spatial axiality. The rooms are vertically integrated by diagonal sightlines from one level to another. The opening in the floor creates an imaginary space that connects the top and bottom floors with the intermediate entry level. In this space, the vertical axis is crossed by a direction outwards through the window wall towards the vast space of the exterior.

Interior of four-bedroom apartment, upper living room.

Section of four-bedroom apartment. Scale 1:200.

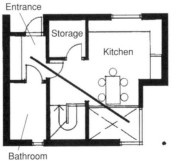

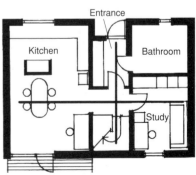

Axiality and drawings of the entry level, four- and three-bedroom apartments. Furnishing schemes from interviews. Scale 1:200.

The three-bedroom apartments have a longitudinal axis that connects the dining room, the landing at the top of the stairs and a bedroom – three rooms with different shapes. A door separates the bedroom from the landing, which is open to the dining room. The same apartment also has a short transverse axis that connects three small rooms, a circulation zone comprising the entrance hall, landing and stairs.

Enclosure

The Hestra apartments are characterized by a feeling of spatial openness. This applies to the interior and exterior alike. Traditionally enclosed bedrooms are set in sharp contrast to open and dynamic spaces. The openness increases successively from closed private rooms through open dining and living rooms to the expansive imaginary exterior space that surrounds the home.

The most closed in spaces are the ground-floor bedrooms. Their openings are few and small. The bedrooms on the top floor have a more open character with ribbon windows under the eaves and a greater spatial volume due to their cathedral ceilings. Stopping the walls short of the roof reduces their function to that of space-defining screens.

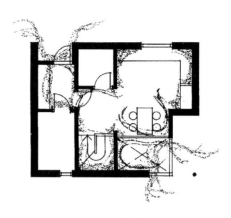

The apartment's enclosure, marked in heavy lines, entry level of four-bedroom apartment. Scale 1:200.

The open rooms (kitchen, dining room and living room) are separated from adjoining spaces by partial boundaries such as banks of cabinets and wall fragments. These open rooms have dynamic forms that are accentuated vertically by the openings between the floors. Broad expanses of glass dissolve the boundary between the interior and the natural space outside, allowing each to penetrate the other. These large openings dominate the surface of the exterior walls. At the gable ends, the windows wrap around corners, further strengthening the openness of the space.

The opening in the floors creates an openness among the interior spaces of the apartment. The architect explained how this spatial integration increases the social integration of the home:

> You can hear each other. Is that him walking up there? Is Dad up there smoking his pipe? This kind of thing establishes the rules of social behaviour, you know – for better or worse.
>
> (Personal interview, Jens Arnfred, architect)

The design of this opening, with large windows passing through two storeys to the floor below, helps define a space on the border between inside and out. The walls seem to float above the ground, and the

Floor opening and the large glazed opening facing natural landscape. Picture of two-bedroom apartment from living room on upper floor. Photo: Ulf Nilsson.

natural landscape is allowed to flow right into the building. The interior spaces consciously open to the outside. The architect's vision was for the life inside the building to be advertised, to become part of the activity of the exterior space. The living room and kitchen are social spaces that work together with the exterior, intended to encourage social interaction among the residents.

> The relationship between the people in the buildings and the natural environment was a point of departure. That's a very conscious thing. It's not just a matter of putting up a wall, or just a fence. We've never been particularly interested in privacy like that. Alternatively, privacy can be incredibly important, and you need to provide space for it. But the public things – everyday life, food, eating, being with people – of course these things can happen right along with the life outside through open connections – but not too open.
>
> (Personal interview, Jens Arnfred)

The entrance from the courtyard space into the interior of the apartment follows two sequences of spaces, one at the front door and the other at the door to the terrace. The entrance niche is a semi-private space, forming the exterior part of the border between inside and out. The niche clarifies the penetration of the entrance through the facade and accentuates the role of the wall as a protective shell for the interior. The niche

Imaginary spaces in front of facade.

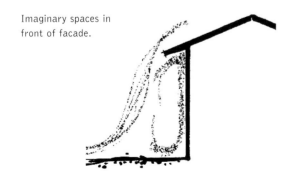

Bedroom, ribbon window under the eaves.
Photo: Sten Gromark.

offsets and extends the join between public and private spheres, to avoid them meeting abruptly at the front door threshold. The second border sequence occurs in the opening in the floor that joins two levels.

Deep niches and broadly overhanging roofs form imaginary semi-private outdoor rooms along the facade. The delineation of space is strongest under the projecting balconies at the gable ends, and these spaces interact with the interior through the large windows. Residents seldom commented on enclosure during our interviews, rarely using the terms 'open' and 'closed'; instead their observations dealt with the consequences of openness and enclosure. This is how Niklas indicated his appreciation for the openness of his apartment:

> All these windows bring you close to nature. No matter where you sit and look out you see birds right outside the windows.
>
> (Personal interview (Niklas), Niklas and Lena, four-bedroom apartment residents)

In the following quotation Nina describes how the size of the windows influences the relationship between inside and out:

Choreographed movement;
example from four-bedroom
apartment, entry level.
Scale 1:200.

1. Anticipation
2. Accumulation
3. Surprise

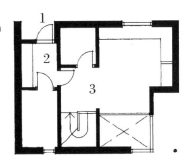

In the fall, when the rowanberries ripen, sometimes when I look out it seems every last window is like a painting. It's beautiful. I feel like nature is inside my apartment, both because it's built with a lot of natural materials and because of the great openness outward with all of these windows. Yes, it's diffuse: am I inside or am I outside?

(Personal interview, Nina, two-bedroom apartment resident)

Movement

There are two clearly distinguishable movements in the Hestra apartments. The first movement has been choreographed by the architect and comprises three phases: *anticipation*, *accumulation* and *surprise*. The character of each of the three spaces involved is clarified by the contrast from one to the next and by the movement through them. The sequence I have chosen as an example comes from one of the four-bedroom units. The movement involves dramatic changes between relative darkness and brightness, between enclosed and open space.

Choreographed movement in three steps.
Anticipation. Accumulation. Surprise.
Photo (*bottom*): Sten Gromark.

- *Anticipation* begins outside, at the front door. The space outside is vast, light-filled and bounded only by imaginary borders. The niche directs our attention to the front door set within it.
- *Accumulation* happens in the completely enclosed hallway, where the only source of daylight is the small round window set in the front door. Two doorways lead on from here. The hall is the interior part of the

border zone between inside and out. From the hall one can glimpse the interior of the apartment, but there is yet another threshold, one more boundary to cross.

- *Surprise*, the objective of this sequence of movements, comes when we enter the large, brightly lit, and dynamic space beyond. The contrast from the small, dimly lit, closed hallway is strong and clear.

The second movement in the apartment is vertical, and is most clear in the three-level units. The opening in the floors connects the different levels along a vertical axis. The adjacent stairway offers the chance to move from one floor to the next. The three-level apartments have a small opening in the wall that surrounds the stairs that bring the space of the stairwell into contact with the space of the void in the floors and establishes a relationship between the two.

The gradual ascent of the stairs is broken at each floor, where both the rhythm and the vertical movement are broken. By enclosing the stairwell, the architect focuses attention on the space revealed at each floor – the goal of the movement – rather than the ascent of the stairs.

Spatial figure

The spatial figures of the Hestra apartments correspond in many ways to the nomenclature of the predominant standard Functionalist apartment. The largest room in the four-bedroom unit is the living room, at $19m^2$ (204 sq ft), just smaller than the $20m^2$ (215 sq ft) prescribed by housing standards. Its medium-sized rooms are the $12m^2$ (129 sq ft) bedroom and the $15m^2$ (161 sq ft) kitchen. The rest of the spaces are small, with areas of 3 to $5m^2$ (32–54 sq ft).

The spatial figure of the rooms varies from one apartment type to the next. In the three-bedroom apartments, the bedrooms have a clearly rectangular shape with the proportions 3:4. This shape recurs in the larger rooms – dining room, kitchen and living room – as well as the smaller hallway. There are a couple of areas

Living room on upper floor of four-bedroom apartment.
Photo: Ulf Nilsson.

with near square shapes that form sub-spaces within the larger rooms, for example the eating area of the kitchen and the place next to the floor opening in the living room. In contrast to the rooms' similarity in shape, they differ in a number of ways such as ceiling form, fenestration, degree of openness and direction.

The architect designed these rooms intuitively, without the use of a theory of proportion:

> Actually we only design from the heart. We don't completely clarify the concepts. We're not thorough in that way, but we do like to arrange space and we're pretty good at that aspect of design. But there aren't words for everything, you know what I mean? We don't always know exactly what we're doing. There's always an element of both spontaneity and surprise.
>
> (Personal interview, Jens Arnfred, architect)

In the four-bedroom units, the proportional ratio 0:85 dominates. This ratio can be found in the bedrooms, part of the living room, even the outside dimensions of the apartment. The remaining rooms have a width-to-length ratio of 0.7. A void in the gable end creates dynamic spaces at the ground-floor kitchen and dining room and the living areas on other levels. The dynamics of these rooms stem from the interaction between various rectangular room shapes. The large opening in the facade and the vertical opening between floors infuse the apartment with dynamism and daylight.

Daylight

The play of daylight is one of the most prominent and significant influences on our perception of the Hestra apartments. It is one of the aspects upon which residents commented appreciatively. Niklas said of the upper living area:

> If you ever wanted to sit and watch soccer on a Saturday afternoon and the sun was really shining you could barely see the TV. But there's also a positive aspect to that, to the fact that it's so bright here, the walls are white, and we don't have curtains. That means we get a tremendous amount of light compared to what you get in a conventional building.
> (Personal interview (Niklas), Niklas and Lena, four-bedroom apartment residents)

The daylight illuminance here varies between relatively high levels – between bright and extremely bright rooms. The space in the opening between levels is the brightest in the apartment. It is followed in order of decreasing illuminance by the dining area, the somewhat less bright kitchen, the bedrooms, and finally the hall, which is the apartment's dimmest space. The daylight in the rooms that the architect calls 'social spaces' is stronger than in the more enclosed, private bedrooms. Contrasting daylight levels create differing characters and qualities for each room and each area of the apartment.

The space in the opening between floors is important to the daylighting scheme. The tall and broad window walls provide a great wash of daylight. In addition the room is shallow, so incoming light is effectively reflected by the surrounding white walls and the stair wall and solid rails. The abundance of direct daylight is intensified by this reflected light, which is thrown back into the interior of the space.

Many of the residents made reference to their appreciation of the daylight in this space, which opens to the outdoors. For Karin, 'the light and the location, with nature right outside', formed an important first impression of the Hestra apartment.

All of the larger apartments here have a transverse axis extending from the entrance to the space in the

Living room on ground floor of four-bedroom apartment.
Photo: Ulf Nilsson.

opening between floors. The drama of this feature is due in large part to the contrasting intensity of daylight from one room to the next along the axis. The sequence is orchestrated to provide a pleasant surprise as one moves from darkness into light, from the dimly lit hall to the bright light of the floor opening.

The windows have simple, rectangular profiles, so their detailing does not significantly articulate the incoming light.

The space in the opening between the floors and that of the entrance are polar opposites that dominate

Kitchen in one-bedroom apartment.
Photo: Ulf Nilsson.

the daylighting of the apartment. The brightness and openness of the former is critical to its character of occupying the border between inside and out.

Organization of spaces

The light and airy Hestra apartments include many of the identifying characteristics of the Functionalist home. The plans employ a circulation system with neutral hubs surrounded by dead-end rooms. In the vertical circulation pattern, a stair connects small ante-rooms from which all other spaces can be entered. An examination of the furnished plan reveals little flexibility in the use of the various rooms, except in the four-bedroom units. Each room is dedicated to a specific function such as sleeping or socializing. The three levels of the four-bedroom apartments, however, offer several alternatives. Their furnished plans show a horizontally divided organization, with the entrance level and kitchen providing the social and geographic heart of the home. The parents use the uppermost level, the children the lowest. Each has a living area that adjoins the bedrooms.

The relationship of each building to the site is of great importance to its architectural expression and to

Space in the floor opening. View from four-bedroom apartment dining area down towards living room on ground floor.

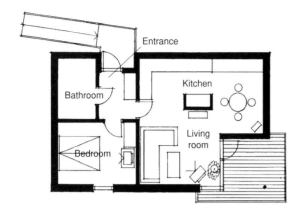

Furnishing schemes from interviews.
One- and three-bedroom apartments.
Scale 1:200.

the residents' perceptions of their homes. The buildings are carefully nestled into a forested landscape, arranged around spatially open courtyards. The architect has striven to find a resonance between the buildings and the natural landscape:

> In Sweden of course there are many kinds of landscapes, such fantastic landscapes. But in Denmark we have so few that we have to make the most of what we've got. Danish buildings grow out of the landscape. The building and landscape are supposed to speak the same language, share the same attitude, each leading naturally to the other.
>
> (Personal interview, Jens Arnfred, architect)

These buildings reinterpret traditional Scandinavian architecture, working in concert with the surrounding environment. Stone fences and old gravel paths have been preserved, and it is only a short distance to trails for walking in the woods or jogging. Despite the obviously modern appearance of the buildings, they reminded Olle of the country home of his youth:

> Well I guess it's Mother Nature. In the summer it's completely different, you know. It's fantastic, I get those real . . . feelings from my childhood – I was born in the country. It smells good, the birds sing. You get the feeling you're in . . . well not exactly Pippi Longstocking's village, but something like that. You can see culture preserved in the natural landscape – they haven't torn down the old stone fences.
>
> (Personal interview (Olle), Ollie and Petra, three-bedroom apartment residents)

The buildings and the grounds around them are ordered by a gradation in the degree of privacy. The area is divided into four clearly delineated levels, becoming increasingly intimate as one proceeds from the public space to the edge that separates the private interior of the home from the exterior.

The first level comprises the complex as a whole, in which two groups of buildings radiate from a pair of oak-covered hillocks, one to the north and one to the south. This complex is clearly distinguishable from the surrounding natural environment. Nina described for me the relationship between the area and its setting:

> Actually I now think it's completely ingenious to build this way, with black [corrugated cladding] and the natural landscape, and placing the buildings in the landscape so that you preserve a great deal of it. So now the buildings really appeal to me, especially in the evening, when the tall glass facades glow—they're really beautiful then.
>
> (Personal interview, Nina, two-bedroom apartment resident)

The second level in the sequence of increasing intimacy comprises the courtyard spaces between the buildings. The courtyard of the southern group is an overgrown lawn that slopes to the south, gradually transiting into the natural landscape. Each courtyard includes several small trees and bushes. The northern group is sited on more gently sloping terrain, so that only two of the six buildings have three-level apartments.

The third level is made up of a system of walking paths that lead to the entrance of each apartment. These paths closely follow the facades, passing just outside the kitchen windows, occupying the imaginary spaces that adjoin each facade beneath the broadly overhanging edge of the roof.

The fourth and most private level of the grounds comprises the entrance niches and residents' private outdoor rooms. The entrance to each apartment is emphasized by recessing it into the volume of the building, a symbolic step towards the private sphere of the home. Each apartment's outdoor room lies just outside of its window wall, giving it direct contact with the interior. The private space of the interior meets its surroundings through the vertical space of the opening between floors. This space occupies the border between

Furnishing scheme from interview. Four-bedroom apartment. From above: upper floor, intermediate entry level and ground floor. Scale 1:200.

Furnishing scheme from interview.
Four-bedroom apartment.
Scale 1:200.

the spatial poles of inside and out. The large glass surfaces provide an open and interpretable interface between the natural landscape and the space of the interior.

These spatial formations and delineations, together with the sensitive approach to the siting of the buildings, are important elements in the process by which residents appropriate their homes:

> All of it's ours [said Nina, laughing], but it feels . . . more like it belongs to everyone than just to us. And then there's the courtyard, which is shared by the four buildings here on the south hill.
> (Personal interview, Nina, two-bedroom apartment resident)

The sequential delineation of exterior space allows the residents gradually to establish personal territory outside of their homes:

> I guess the idea was that we would all use these areas as a kind of communal ground. But we don't really – it gets divided naturally. You don't go out and lounge right in front of the neighbour's place, and so forth.
> (Personal interview (Niklas), Niklas and Lena, four-bedroom apartment residents)

The design of the home is an important factor in how residents establish contact with the courtyard and with their neighbours. Every room in the apartment has a view of the courtyard. The openness of these apartments allows the residents to see one another and connect each unit with the faces of its individual residents. Niklas described what it's like to stand at the sink and do the dishes:

> When you stand here, you can see all these neighbours, you know. Maybe subconsciously you think, Now he just got home, and What are they doing? and so forth. You don't see that in a normal

apartment building in the same way. Usually you shut yourself in.

(Personal interview (Niklas), Niklas and Lena, four-bedroom apartment residents)

The design of the private space inside each apartment prepares its residents to meet the space outside. The close proximity of each building to the next offers a limited type of view from the courtyard into the apartments and vice versa. Residents can also see from one apartment into another across the courtyard. But none of those interviewed saw this as particularly negative; on the contrary, most thought it was good to be able to see if their neighbours were at home. Exposure is limited by the leaves on the trees, by shadows, and by the high sills of the windows. Still, Niklas and Lena had different opinions on the visual openness of the apartments:

Niklas: With the space between buildings and all of these trees we're extremely closed in here. At first you felt like . . . since you can see out, in the beginning you thought people could see in, and we were going to have blinds in here and up there. And then these windows that start at chest height – of course you see both into and out of a window – at first I guess it felt like they could see me, but of course they don't. Maybe just a little glimpse.
Lena: I guess I still feel that way today, that people are watching me sometimes.

(Personal interview, Lena and Niklas, four-bedroom apartment residents)

The apartment's visual exposure to the outside is concentrated primarily in the space in the opening between floors. The dining area in the four-bedroom units is located to one side of this glazed opening and the stairway is enclosed by a wall. A balcony limits the exposure of the upper living room. Nina, a resident in one of the two-bedroom units, described her feelings about the apartment's exposure:

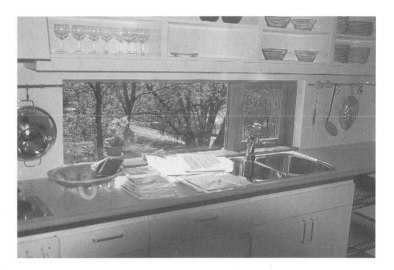

'When you stand here, you can see all these neighbours, you know. Maybe subconsciously you think, "Now he just got home", and "What are they doing?" and so forth. You don't see that in a normal apartment building in the same way. Usually you shut yourself in'. (Personal interview (Niklas), Niklas and Lena, four-bedroom apartment residents. Photo: Sten Gromark.

Building meets site. Photo from the northern group of buildings.

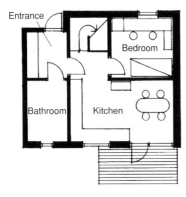

Furnishing scheme from interview. Two-bedroom apartment.
Scale 1:200.

Yes, but you're really only exposed on the ground floor – the stairway is covered, and there are only two small windows. You never see the kitchen; possibly from the side. The top floor of course is protected by the railing around the deck. So all in all I think the architect succeeded. But still you feel like you're really exposed.

(Personal interview, Nina, two-bedroom apartment resident)

Some of the apartment's detailing opens it to the outside, some elements screen it in. For example, the gable-end apartments have two private outdoor rooms, a balcony on the upper level that is visually protected and an entirely open area at grade level outside the glass wall. Residents can choose between the two, and Karin, who enjoys socializing with her neighbours, often sits out on the ground-floor terrace:

Yeah, we're not really the type to shut ourselves in, like 'No, we want to be alone, so let's go sit up there where we can be sure to be left in peace'. We're not like that. It's much more fun to sit down there.

(Personal interview, Karin, four-bedroom apartment resident)

Lena and Niklas make more use of the upper balcony because 'the balcony is "built in" and you can sit up there and eat; we think it's very cozy' (personal interview (Niklas), Niklas and Lena, four-bedroom apartment residents).

The openness between the apartments and the courtyard gives neighbours and courtyard activities an identity. Residents can, step-by-step, identify themselves through the multi-level structure and boundaries of the public areas. Nina described her impression of the courtyard as follows:

I'm so sloppy sometimes, you know, but still I can feel a greater sense of responsibility since I started living here. I can pick up trash out here because it suddenly bothers me. I don't know if I'm getting older or if it's that you do feel a certain responsibility in a place like this. You like the way it is, and you just want it to look nice.

(Personal interview, Nina, two-bedroom apartment resident)

The way the residents use the outdoor spaces and voluntarily look after the courtyard are examples of how people mark the territory where they feel they belong. An old oak tree stands just off the gable end of one building, and the family who had the apartment within took great care of 'their' tree:

We have made it clear to everyone that we don't want kids coming and sitting on the branches so that they break off. There are huge trees all over the place here, and there is no need for them to climb this particular one.

(Personal interview (Niklas), Niklas and Lena, four-bedroom apartment residents)

One consequence of defining boundaries in the public space is that it provides a social life among these buildings which comes with a certain freedom of choice: residents can choose whether they want to be alone or socialize with their neighbours; they can meet in the courtyard, though there are also places with varying degrees of privacy; and they can see and be seen without further commitment. Niklas asserted the value of being able to choose the intensity of one's neighbourhood socializing:

You can go in and borrow stuff, and people pitch in to clean out the undergrowth and so forth. It's on the kind of level where each person decides how much he puts into it. A lot of times when you come home from work there's always someone out here doing something. Sometimes you're too tired to chat, more than just to say hi. But you can always stop and talk if you want.

(Personal interview (Niklas), Niklas and Lena, four-bedroom apartment residents)

The freedom to choose also extends to the relationship between visitors and residents. The entrance portals and the path through the area allow visitors to enter the courtyard without disclosing their intentions. The portals diminish the privacy of the courtyard by giving strangers access. The presence of strangers in the courtyard strengthens the sense of freedom from forced social obligations.

Another important aspect of the process by which residents appropriate their homes is their appreciation for the natural environment that characterizes the area. Nature means a lot to these residents. Wild grass, heather and cowberry bushes grow right up to the buildings. Residents can interpret the sensitivity with which the landscape has been preserved as a sign that the architect and builder were concerned for their well-being. The area is quiet and peaceful, and the forest air is fresh. According to Olle: 'being able to sleep with the windows open and wake up to birdsong – no cars, no traffic, and so much oxygen-rich air –is almost priceless' (personal interview (Olle), Olle and Petra, three-bedroom apartment residents).

The proximity to nature has both practical and symbolic aspects. Children's play areas are safe. For Niklas and Lena, nature plays an important role in their way of life:

It's incredibly close. The kids play soccer down here, you know. I don't want to say that you couldn't find a better place to live – I'm sure you could – but for our way of life, we like to be outdoors and go running and stuff. We think this is a fantastic way to live.

(Personal interview (Niklas), Niklas and Lena, four-bedroom apartment residents)

The architect's sensitive approach to the property has also preserved something of the history of the place. The surrounding space, the space of nature, can be understood as part of a comprehensible historical context. The history of the site is manifest in the new buildings. This offers yet another resource for the creation of identity. Conservation of the site was an important aspect of the design process for the architect:

We are just visitors here, we've only borrowed this landscape. We feel like somehow we've just come to this wood for a visit. That gives the place a delicacy, an airiness, a lightness, and we also think that in a way it's nice that buildings break down. They shouldn't have to be blasted away. We are only visitors on this earth.

(Personal interview, Jens Arnfred, architect)

Arnfred's adaptation of the buildings to their site helps residents create identity and gain insight into their living situation.

The Hestra apartments show many signs of a successful process of appropriation. Some residents spoke of a feeling of community and pride at living in 'the

Living room on ground floor, four-bedroom apartment.
Photo: Ulf Nilsson.

Danish buildings' at Hestra. This despite the fact that, according to Lars, many of the local inhabitants find the appearance of the buildings difficult to accept:

> Everyone thinks at first that they look like barns. I thought so, too ... but you get used to it. Now I think they're very good looking, they don't look like the average apartment building. And that's good, I don't see that as something negative. I think this is one of the nicer neighbourhoods in Borås.
> (Personal interview, Lars, one-bedroom apartment resident)

Similar stories were revealed in other interviews as well, stories of how outsiders find it hard to accept the look of the buildings and of how much the residents themselves appreciate them:

> It's probably about the buildings, when it comes down to it, because I don't think the average Jones's want to move in here, they're the type that have a problem with these buildings. I guess the people who live here are a little unusual, not all cast from the same mould.
> (Personal interview, Karin, four-bedroom apartment resident)

The residents at Hestra are satisfied with their living situation. They have an intimate and strikingly conscious relationship to the situation and to their homes. Many of them told of how they longed for the spring (the interviews were held on cold and snowy days in February) and for the life they share with their neighbours outdoors.

Case study Norrköping

Description

Case study Norrköping examines three two- and three-bedroom apartments in the Vattenkonsten block on the periphery of the old stone centre of Norrköping. The building was designed by Bengt Lindroos and finished in 1987.

The building in question occupies the southwest corner site of the block. The west side of the block faces Hamntorget, a public square, and the inner part of the town's harbour. A main road separates the square from the harbour. The south side faces a vacant site that is being used for parking. A branch of Motala River lies to the north.

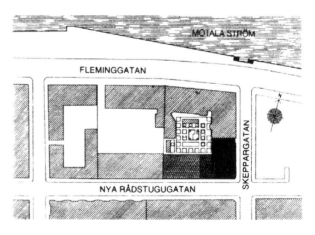

Masterplan. Illustration from Bengt Lindroos, *Och så vidare . . .* (And so on . . ., in Swedish only), International Forlag, Stockholm, 1989.

One enters Lindroos' building from Nya Rådstugu-gatan, through a portal that leads to two stairways and a courtyard shared by the entire block. The building is six storeys high towards the square and four to six storeys towards the street. The ground floor is occupied by commercial space.

The building's structure is a cast-in-place concrete frame with double-width red brick exterior bearing walls and a metal roof.

The apartments are spacious. The large two-bedroom units, with an area of about 98m^2 (1055 sq ft), can be converted to three bedrooms. On the top floor, in the attic, there are several smaller one-bedroom apartments. The apartments have a courtyard side and a street side that are separated by an indirectly lit central area. The courtyard side holds the bedroom and kitchen, while the street side is occupied by a large living area that can be subdivided into smaller rooms. Between them lie the hall, bathroom and toilet, corridor and a walk-in cupboard.

> It's almost always the case that the site, the location, the surroundings tell you what it should be like. Even if you start from the other end, the way I did here, you're still controlled by the site.
>
> (Personal interview, Bengt Lindroos, architect)

I chose the Norrköping apartments for their beautiful planning, and based on their description in various journals and books. The architect is renowned for his residential work, and this also influenced my choice. My personal impressions of the building closely matched my expectations. I particularly appreciated the living room's bay window, the axiality and spatial organization of the plan, and the beautiful facades.

Materials and detailing

In this building, materials play a passive role in the residents' perceptions of their homes. When I asked Siri if she was dissatisfied with anything in her apartment she pointed to the poor quality of the floor in the hall:

The Vattenkonsten block, photo from town square.

> The main thing I can think of would be the floors, because our last place had such handsome floors. Especially in the hallway we should have had hardwood flooring. I guess I think that was a mistake. This apartment is pretty formal, so you want it to be a little stylish. It's a little disappointing to come in and see cork flooring.
>
> (Personal interview, Siri, two-bedroom apartment resident)

Likewise I had to press Rut with leading questions before she would criticize the apartment's materials or detailing:

> I just think it's so nice to have hardwood floors. I really would have liked to have had that in the bedroom, too. It's okay to have linoleum in the hall and kitchen, because you get more wear and tear there. But I wouldn't mind a wood floor in the bedroom, clean and fresh.
>
> (Personal interview, Rut, one-bedroom apartment resident)

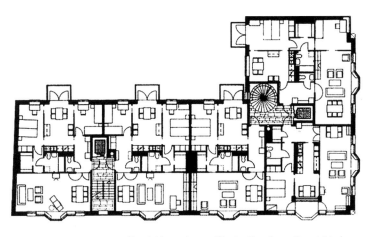

Furnishing scheme. Illustration from Bengt Lindroos,
Och så vidare . . . (And so on . . . , in Swedish only),
International Forlag, Stockholm, 1989.

The materials specified for these apartments are above average, but not remarkable or unique in any way. The floors in the smaller bedrooms are linoleum or vinyl, while the living rooms have hardwood. The trims around floors, windows and doors are of standard dimensions, factory painted, and without mitred corner joints. Most of the architectural woodwork is also prefabricated and shop-painted. The walls are papered and the smooth ceilings are painted white.

One detail, however, that clearly means a lot to residents is the living room's bay window. This welcoming and inviting touch made a strong impression on many residents during their first visits to the apartments. Ture told me: 'When we came in and saw that window, the bay window, ah it's so charming' (personal interview (Ture), Ture and Sandra, two-bedroom apartment residents).

Vera appreciated the deep stone-clad niche of the bay window:

You know, that's something we missed in our last apartment. We had small window sills held up by flimsy little brackets. Here we've got marble that sits tight to the wall.

(Personal interview (Vera), Vera and Ulf,
two-bedroom apartment residents)

Another detail praised by the residents was the sliding doors between the bedrooms and kitchen. Ture had practical reasons, saying, 'This place is great: you can slide those doors closed while you cook, and yet they're not in the way [when they're open]'. (Personal interview (Ture), Ture and Sandra, two-bedroom apartment residents.)

However, many found the multitude of doors into the kitchen impractical. Ulf and Vera had put up a shelf in front of the sliding door nearest the facade. Vera told me: 'There are a little too many doors. But you can fix that yourself – just close one of the passageways' (personal interview (Vera), Vera and Ulf, two-bedroom apartment residents).

Bay window, detail.

Living room bay window.

Several other details also drew complaints. Ulf and Vera were dissatisfied with the size of the balcony, the width of the balcony doors, and the trim around the doors. Vera voiced her husband's frustration: 'That balcony really bothers you, you say that almost every time, that it could have been a little bit longer' (personal interview (Vera), Vera and Ulf, two-bedroom apartment residents).

For her part, Vera found it difficult to accept the trim details in the apartment:

> The corners over the doors aren't mitred. Sometimes I look at that when I'm lying in bed. The trim looks so cheap. It's sad. Mitred corners give a completely different impression, you know. It does a whole lot for the appearance.
>
> (Personal interview (Vera), Vera and Ulf,
> two-bedroom apartment residents)

It is certain that it is the architectural details, rather than the materials chosen, that are important to the residents of the Norrköping apartments in helping them to initiate the process of appropriation.

Axiality

Longitudinal and transverse sightlines and axes are important to the impression of the Norrköping apartments. From one room contrasts in light and room shapes in the adjoining rooms can be observed. Directional and circulation axes are also important to how one moves through and perceives the opportunities for

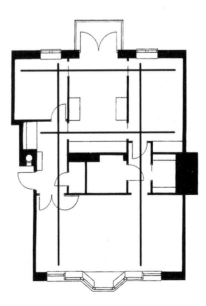

The apartment's axiality. Scale 1:200.

Transverse axis, view of the hallway and the little bedroom from the living room.

The two transverse axes stretch from facade to facade, each from a bedroom window across the hall or corridor to either side of the living room's bay window. These axes are quite long, touching three rooms with different materials, spatial figures and functions. There are also differences in the openings between rooms. The doors to the bedrooms are standard size, while the living room is entered through double doors set in a broad, rectangular archway. The bedrooms and living room are asymmetrically grouped about the axes, while the passageway is symmetrically divided about an axis that cuts through the middle of it.

The courtyard side has two very different longitudinal axes. The more interior axis stretches from a bedroom through a sliding door, along the kitchen work surface, and into the hall. The other follows along the facade, illuminated by daylight from one bedroom to the other, passing by the wide balcony doors as it crosses through the kitchen. These longitudinal axes differ from the transverse in that they are shorter, they connect less important points and pass through smaller openings. The long and narrow living room suggests a subtle third longitudinal axis along its length. The architect has pointed out that 'One quality is that the longitudinal axis in the living room is parallel to the facade, which is what inspired the form of the big window'.[3]

The entrance offers no overview of the apartment. One must first move along the axial system, around the dimly lit central part; only then can one understand the layout of the place. Each axis reveals a limited portion of the apartment.

Enclosure

Two important features break through the wall that separates the private space of the interior from the public world outside: the living room's bay window and the balcony on to which the kitchen opens. The stepped form of the bay window, its central panel reaching to the floor, and the offset of the small outermost windows call attention to the thickness and mass of the wall. Standing in the bay window, one can look back along

movement through the three parts – street side, centre and courtyard side.

The architect worked consciously with axiality in planning these apartments:

[The axiality] is obvious and conscious. Just looking at the floor plans like this, [the axes] seem equally important. But if you imagine closing this one sliding door into the kitchen, it gives the kitchen a completely different, uninteresting character. It's extremely important that [the movement] happens where the light is.

(Personal interview, Bengt Lindroos, architect)

the facade at the outside of the building. Here the significance of the border between interior and exterior space is made clear.

The balconies allow residents to move out physically into the exterior space that surrounds the home. The semi-private balconies are placed in the semi-public courtyard and create a transition from the private interior to the public realm. They also provide another opportunity to see the outside of the building. The enclosure of the intimate space inside is clarified and contrasted by the boundless expanse outside. The home thus becomes a solid, safe starting point for the individual's identification even in the public realm.

Enclosed spaces dominate the interior. The courtyard side seems more enclosed than the street side. The smaller bedroom's openings are concentrated at the two corners towards the kitchen and hall; the interior of the room has nothing to counter the feeling of enclosure. The fact that the window is small and pressed to the outer surface of the facade underscores the sense of enclosure. Its deep niche emphasizes the thickness of the outside walls and their enclosing capacity.

Dining area and the door out to the balcony.

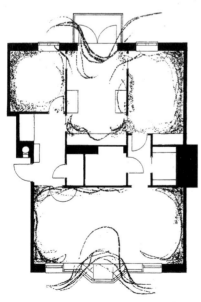

The apartment's enclosure, marked in heavy lines.
Scale 1:200.

The larger bedroom also has a clear shape. It has the same window arrangement as the smaller. Its closets are built into a niche by the door, allowing that wall to work together with the others to form a whole. The placement of the bedrooms' pocket doors in the corners gives the impression of moveable wall planes that can be adjusted to regulate the degree of openness and enclosure.

The open kitchen provides a contrast to the two bedrooms. It has a broad and tall pair of French doors that lead out to the balcony, the expanse of the doors making the surrounding wall seem like merely a frame for the opening. The kitchen opens to the courtyard. At the corners of the room, four sliding doors diminish the sense of enclosure that the solid corners create. The kitchen works together with the adjacent rooms.

The openings in the living room are arranged with a rough symmetry. The wide door openings are shifted slightly off-centre, and the bay window composition marks the perceived centreline of the room. Strong corners and broad expanses of uninterrupted wall

The apartment's light. Bay window in the living room.
Photo: Sune Sundahl.

the architect has gone back in time to get more space and light. When we come home from our friends', where it's cramped and shabby, this whole apartment just opens up for you.

(Personal interview (Vera), Vera and Ulf, two-bedroom apartment residents)

In the centre of the apartment, passageways and areas 'with water' separate one side from the other. The passageways are oblong spaces with lots of large openings. Their openness to the courtyard and street clarifies their role as connecting spaces.

None of the residents interviewed considered any of the rooms markedly open. There is a certain openness and spaciousness in the living room, and this is perhaps what Ture was getting at when he said, 'I for one think this is a really cozy place to live, and at the same time light and airy. There's certainly a nice feeling to the place' (personal interview (Ture), Ture and Sandra, two-bedroom apartment residents).

The dynamism of the street-side bay window contrasts with the calmness of the side towards the courtyard. Vera offered the following comment:

The room that's mine, the larger bedroom, feels cozy and safe. But I've never had the feeling that the living room was too big. The kitchen is in the middle, yes that's right, right between the big, bright place and my safe little nook.

(Personal interview (Vera), Vera and Ulf, two-bedroom apartment residents)

Movement

A variety of possibilities for movement makes the Norrköping apartments expressive. These movements are characterized by a wide variation. There are different circuit opportunities, a formal sequence and axial movements the rhythms of which vary with the size and brightness of the spaces they cross.

One can walk a loop through rooms with varying daylight conditions, sizes and functions, and through

clearly support the sense of enclosure. The bay window dominates the space, its form accentuated where it pushes through the exterior wall. The openness of the room's central feature contrasts with the enclosing character of the rest.

Vera describes how it feels to come home to her apartment:

There's a little forward thinking in this apartment, you know. We have good friends that live in a building from the 1960s where you come into a little hall and then all the rooms are small. So I guess here

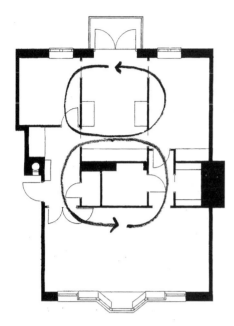

Possible circulation loops.
Scale 1:200.

all three areas of the apartment. The two longitudinal axes on the courtyard side offer some freedom of choice, and the one along the windows stretches the full length of the apartment. The circulation loop gives the place greater flexibility and expands the mix of impressions by integrating various visual and circulation axes from one room to another.

The strong differences between transverse axes in terms of room size, daylight and function add drama and rhythm to the movements.

The living room's bay window is a visual goal for the movement from darkness to light and an example of how bright spaces encourage movement.

The axes make it possible to move through the apartment in a variety of ways, and to gather a variety of impressions. This plethora of possible movements, however, can be contrary to the functional suitability of

Bay window in
the living room.
Photo: Sune
Sundahl.

the home. Ture and Sandra, for example, chose to close off one of the transverse axes. As Sandra told me, they preferred to use one of the passageways for storage:

> Because it's not necessary at all to be able to go through there. We closed that off immediately. If you have company or even if it's just us in the living room there's no real reason to go through that way. It's just a bathroom and a storage closet, and you normally use those passageways from the bedroom anyway, since there's also an extra bath in the hall.
> (Personal interview (Sandra), Sandra and Ture, two-bedroom apartment residents)

However, both Sandra and Ture appreciate the two longitudinal axes in the kitchen. Maybe these were the basis for their decision to use the little bedroom as a dining room and keep the kitchen free of furniture. The openness between the kitchen and the two adjacent bedrooms provides a practical and flexible relationship, as Ture described:

> Now sometimes if my wife is standing here working at the kitchen counter and I'm setting the table in the dining room, then I go the other way, along the facade, because it gets pretty tight between the refrigerator, counter, and stove. Why go and crowd each other?
> (Personal interview (Ture), Ture and Sandra, two-bedroom apartment residents)

Unlike Ture and Sandra, Siri liked having the two transverse passageways, and kept them both open. She said they made the rooms seem more open and also allowed for greater flexibility in how one moves through the apartment. When I asked if she would consider closing off one of the passageways, she said firmly, 'I think that would ruin the apartment' (personal interview, Siri, two-bedroom apartment resident).

The circulation loops work together with the system of axes as we alternate between horizontal and longitudinal movements. Architect Bengt Lindroos has attested to the importance of the possibility of walking a circuit through the home:

> If the mark of a good and beautiful home is that you can do the traditional chain dance around the Christmas tree, which is how a construction loan reviewer in the property management office during the 1940s saw it, then these apartments I've designed must be unusually good because in several of them you can dance through up to eight different paths, a wealth of variety which I've never before achieved.[4]

The movements in the Norrköping apartments suggest an older, more formal style of living. A ritualistic movement begins in the hall, where guests are invited into the front part of the living room, which functions in much the same way as the traditional drawing room. They then move to the dining area in the rear of the space for dinner. After dinner they are invited to sit in the parlour (the middle part of the living room). For dinner parties Siri even uses the smaller bedroom next to the kitchen, which she calls 'the blue room', as a smoking chamber or library – where in years past the men often gathered after dinner. She explained that 'This [part of the living room] is like the dining area and we always joke about that little sofa, which we call the *boudoir*' (personal interview, Siri, two-bedroom apartment resident).

The two longitudinal axes on the courtyard side generate a movement from the two bedrooms into the kitchen. This movement goes from smaller to larger spaces, from darker rooms to brighter, and from functionally simple to more dynamic intensely social spaces. The movement through the living room works similarly. The window composition in the centre is the focus of the two transverse axes from courtyard to street, from private interior to public exterior, and of course this bay window is exactly where interior and exterior spaces meet.

The movement from the hall to the living room is also a welcoming gesture. Visitors move from the dimly lit core of the building towards the bright light of the spaces along the facades. Daylight pierces the apartment from one facade to the other along this first transverse axis, so that one is also presented with the courtyard immediately upon entering.

The pace of movement through the apartment varies with the contrasting daylight conditions and room sizes. We move from bright through dark spaces and emerge again into bright daylight. From large rooms we pass through small ones into medium-sized, from there again into small rooms in which we can quickly orient ourselves, and again into larger spaces that make us pause for orientation. The combination of room shapes produces a dramatic impression. The dark and enclosed passageways are in contrast to the bright light and open layout of the living room. The movement from one side of the apartment to the other encompasses varying degrees of enclosure. All of this generates a lively movement with changing rhythm.

Spatial figure

The spatial figures of the Norrköping apartments correspond in many ways to the room types of the typical Functionalist home. The largest is the living room, with an area of about 30m² (325 sq ft), which can be subdivided to give an extra room. The kitchen and bedrooms are medium-sized, 9 to 13m² (100–140 sq ft). The small rooms – the hall, passageways, storage cupboards and bathrooms – have areas of 3 to 7m² (30–75 sq ft).

The square plays a prominent role in the geometry of these apartments. The living room is formed by two squares together, the smaller bedroom is a single square, and the larger bedroom is made up of one large and two small squares combined. The living rooms added to the central areas form a large square, leaving three smaller squares to complete the floor plan.

This compositional strategy is no surprise, given the prevalence of geometry in the past work of Bengt Lindroos. Anders Wilhelmson, who at one time worked with Lindroos, describes Lindroos' relationship to the square as 'a means to create space and volume, not

Bay window, facade facing the street Nya Rådstugugatan.

merely to describe'.[5] This is perhaps an apt characterization of the strong geometry of the plan for the building in question. What we register here are the light, volume, enclosure and connectivity of the spaces. In my interview with him, Lindroos said:

I think that Anders Wilhelmson wrote of the Drottningen block, a residential development I did in Stockholm in 1981, that it was also a strict square scheme before the site softened it up.

(Personal interview, Bengt Lindroos, architect)

Daylight

A primary feature for the perception of daylight in the apartment is the large bay window in the living room. It is engulfed in an intense and lively light, due in part to the fact that the small outermost windows have been drawn in, and to the variation in the height of the sills of the different windows. The middle window, which projects outward, goes all the way to the floor. For the architect, the play of shadows in the window area was important:

> Yes, an essential part of it is that the double-width brick allowed me to pull things in. Like that little window . . . it is extremely effective in the facade, in its shadows, in the composition of shadows and reflections in the canted window panes.
>
> (Personal interview, Bengt Lindroos, architect)

The bay window is a light-filled space that occupies the border region between the private realm of the interior and the public realm of the exterior, and develops the contact between the two. The tall window casts light deep into the shallow room, and the nearby perpendicular wall surface reflects light into the interior.

The character of the daylight varies throughout the apartment. There is the intense south sun in the living room and the more subtle evening light of the courtyard side. There is the contrast between the indirectly lit passageway and hall in the centre of the apartment and the rooms along the facades, which get direct sunshine.

These contrasts in daylight conditions clarify the differences between public and private areas. The living room is both the apartment's brightest room and its most public. The bedrooms are more dimly lit, darker and more private. The varying illuminance in the different rooms also works together with the varying degrees of enclosure in each.

View of hallway and bedroom from living room.

One of the only comments from an interviewee regarding geometry came from Siri, who said, 'The surface area of this place is so . . . geometrically right. I would guess that almost the whole apartment is a square' (personal interview, Siri, two-bedroom apartment resident).

Living room and light cast from bay window.

The passageways in the apartment's dark central area are indirectly lit from two sides with a diffuse light that casts soft shadows.

The windows have simple, rectangular profiles, so the daylight openings are not substantially articulated by the design details.

In my interview with Ulf and Vera we discussed how they moved between courtyard and street sides. Vera always chooses to go from kitchen to living room through the front passageway:

We always go through the passageway, even if it's further. We have the dining table in the living room, but I'm a creature of habit and I go that way anyway. I always think, this is ridiculous, there's another way through, the hallway is much closer when you're carrying plates and food.

(Personal interview (Vera), Vera and Ulf, two-bedroom apartment residents)

When I asked why, she explained that the light is different that way, because she walks towards the light that comes from one of the living room windows.

The daylighting of the Norrköping apartments plays an important role in clarifying the meaningful content in its details and events. The living room's bay window composition provides a strong visual depiction of the breach in the facade and the contact between interior and exterior.

Organization of spaces

The layout of the Norrköping apartment has similarities to the middle-class home of the nineteenth century. It is divided longitudinally into street, centre and courtyard areas. It has rooms that are axially aligned and can be moved through formally and used in a traditional manner. The primary street side is balanced by service areas toward the courtyard; one side is for socializing, one for work and rest.

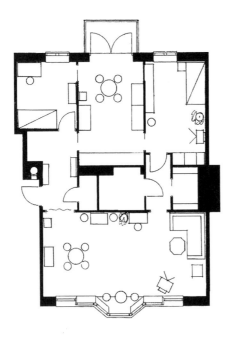

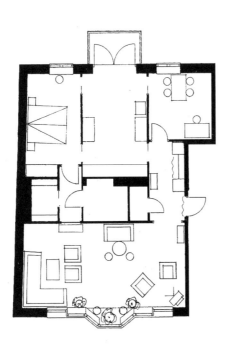

Furnishing schemes from interviews.
Scale 1:200.

However, at the same time the Norrköping apartment satisfies the demands of connectivity and functionality that characterize the Functionalist apartment. It has neutral access to bedrooms, kitchen and living room.

This is clearly an urban building, which distinguishes it from the other case study buildings included here. There are no signs of resident territory outside of the apartments. The courtyard is little used, and it seems that residents regard it primarily as a pretty view from their balconies.

The building's relationship to its site is limited to its connection with the courtyard on one side and the street on the other. The row of rooms facing the courtyard has limited contact with the street, since the central section effectively separates one side from the other. On the street side, the relationship established by the bay window between interior and exterior is extremely significant. The balcony fills the same function on the courtyard side, though in a more reserved manner.

Lindroos described for me how in previous projects he had striven to visually integrate the living room and kitchen. In Norrköping the effect has been the opposite. He explained that 'Everything indicates that the site has been in command of my will, and has given rise to other priorities' (personal interview, Bengt Lindroos, architect).

The residents' use of their apartments demonstrates that the layout allows them to be furnished in a wide variety of ways. There is room for individual interpretation of the rooms. The residents interviewed use their homes to a certain extent in the same way that urban apartments were used a century ago. The large living room provides a setting for different kinds of entertaining and other events.

The ways the residents have furnished their apartments reveals how they perceive this space as comprising three parts – three smaller rooms joined together. One part is a dining room, one the traditional living room with its media centre, and one part a formal sitting area.

In Siri's apartment, the division between public and private leaves each room with some degree of public character. The larger bedroom is the most private space, but it is furnished with several chairs and the placement of the bed is so unobtrusive that the room can work as a natural passage between kitchen and living room when she entertains. The kitchen provides a buffer zone that protects the larger bedroom and also a slightly more private area than the adjacent smaller bedroom. The living room and small bedroom ('the blue room') are the most public areas of Siri's home. Her living room is divided into three parts that correspond to the old middle-class apartment's dining room, parlour and drawing room. She uses both passages between the street and courtyard sides, though the rear passageway by the dining area provides the primary circulation path during parties:

> I usually serve dinner buffet-style from the kitchen, so we go through this way, through the passageway. We can go through the other way, too, through the hall, as long as the wardrobe curtain is closed so you can't see the clothes.
>
> (Personal interview, Siri, two-bedroom apartment resident)

Ture and Sandra have divided their apartment similarly in terms of public and private areas. However, they have chosen to close off the rear passageway with a cabinet. This makes the larger bedroom clearly a private area. The couple used to live in a large house in the country. They wanted to have lots of free space in the kitchen, so they use the smaller bedroom as a dining area. Sandra told me: 'Oh yes, it's so nice, I think, to keep the floor uncluttered . . . better than having a table and chairs in the way all the time' (personal interview (Sandra), Sandra and Ture, two-bedroom apartment residents).

Moving the dining area out of the kitchen to the smaller bedroom has given the kitchen more privacy and the character of a place for work. Ture and Sandra have also divided their living room into three parts. The zone closest to the hall has a corner for watching television; at the other end of the room they have a traditional living room set-up; and the middle area is furnished with vintage pieces that give the impression of a formal sitting room.

In Ulf and Vera's apartment, the living room is the most public space. They each have their own bedrooms, either of which one might walk through on the way to the kitchen. This arrangement dramatically changes the way each room is used. Vera described how they arrived at this scheme:

> First we made the little bedroom into a TV room, but that left the living room empty pretty often. It was crazy to have that beautiful living room so unused. So we moved the TV in there, and now we spend a lot of time in the living room, we really do.
>
> (Personal interview (Vera), Vera and Ulf, two-bedroom apartment residents)

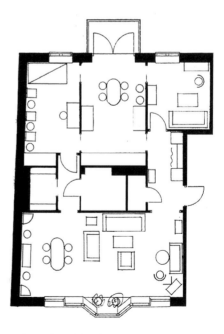

Furnishing scheme from interview.
Scale 1:200.

Like the others, Ulf and Vera divided their living room into three distinct parts: a dining area nearest the entrance, a formal seating arrangement by the bay window to take advantage of the view, and an informal sofa for watching television. The kitchen remains mostly private, though they occasionally sit there with guests. Vera told me, 'We're in the kitchen a lot. I sit here at the kitchen table and work, sewing and writing' (personal interview (Vera), Veral and Ulf, two-bedroom apartment residents).

Rut lives in a one-bedroom apartment on the top floor with a view over Hamntorget Square. Though her apartment is a somewhat reduced version of the others, much is the same. One similarity is the three-part division of the living room. Rut and her housemate have a seating area around the TV at one end, a dining area in the middle, and a kind of look-out spot with a pair of lounge chairs in the other corner. The bedroom is completely separate.

The grounds around the Norrköping building lack the varying degrees of intimacy we have seen in the other case studies. The simple and definitive relationship of this urban apartment building to its street, to the public space of the city, conforms to the traditional pattern. There are no provisions for varying degrees of territorial demarcation in the courtyard. 'There are one or two people who sit down there in the courtyard,' said Siri, 'but otherwise everyone sits up on their balconies' (personal interview, Siri, two-bedroom apartment resident).

The bay window on to the street mediates between the private interior of the apartment and the public space outside, a border zone between inside and out. The residents in the apartments I visited were very fond of just sitting in the bay window and watching events taking place in the street below. 'Oh yes, we sit there sometimes, there in the bay window, and look out, watching everything that moves … curious', said Sandra (personal interview (Sandra), Sandra and Ture, two-bedroom apartment residents).

For these residents, the exterior of the building plays an important role in the process of appropriation. Those I interviewed were proud of the building and its appearance. As Ulf told me:

We're very close [to the centre of town], and yet not right in the midst of it. When you come across Hamnbro bridge it looks very handsome. Lots of

Courtyard facade.

'When you come across the Hamnbro bridge it looks very handsome, you know. Lots of people say
"You live in that beautiful building?". It makes you stand a little bit taller.' (Personal interview (Vera),
Vera and Ulf, two-bedroom apartment residents.) Facade facing Hamntorget.

people say that – "you live in that beautiful building?"
It makes you stand a little bit taller.

> (Personal interview (Ulf), Ulf and Vera,
> two-bedroom apartment residents)

Many residents appreciate the reserved exterior, with its powerful gates, saying it makes them feel safe and secure. Since the stairwells, and particularly the one nearest the street, are shared by only a few apartments, the residents all know one another. But problems arose when others were given permission to use the building's gates and portals. Sandra described the situation:

I don't know if this is relevant, but Ståhls, the property management company, wanted to put up a fence along the border with the neighbouring courtyard, but they weren't allowed to. You're supposed to be able to walk through from that property to this one. The people who live over there walk around on our side a lot. They know our door code and so they have access to our stairwell here. We're a little bit . . . sensitive about that.

> (Personal interview (Sandra),
> Sandra and Ture, two-bedroom
> apartment residents)

The residents are all acquainted with one another, and there is some social interaction among them. Siri's description characterizes the relationship that has developed among neighbours:

> What's good about this [building] is that we're just six families here. We don't have the kind of friendships where we go and ring each other's doorbell – I mean, we don't bother each other that way. We don't exactly chase each other down, it's just a nice balance. We can call each other on the phone if we need help with anything, and that's really great.
>
> (Personal interview, Siri, two-bedroom apartment resident)

Despite the lack of specifically planned meeting points, several of the other residents told of similar relationships with their neighbours.

In general, the residents here are pleased with their living situations, and express their satisfaction in many ways, suggesting a successful appropriation of the home.

Chapter 5

Fields of attributes: a more detailed characterization

We can use comparative analyses and characterizations of how the seven fields of attributes appear in the case studies to discuss the two remaining questions:

- What spatial variables and relationships influence our perception of the non-measurable attributes of residential architecture?
- What deeper significance do non-measurable architectural attributes have for residents?

This discussion is shaped by the theoretical framework presented in Chapter 3 'Identifying fields of attributes', and by the analyses and descriptions in the previous chapter, 'Case studies'. The seven fields of attributes I have identified cannot be given specific dimensions or be definitively determined. However, their criteria and symbolic value can be described through comparative analyses based on the four case studies.

Stumholmen. Window in living room,
looking towards the loggia.
Photo: Göran Peyronson.

Unusual details: window ribbon under the eaves,
pitched roof, glass around corners. The upper
living room in four-bedroom apartment in Hestra.
Photo: Sten Gromark.

The discussion is summarized for each field of attributes in a few general criteria that I consider important to the perception of the non-measurable architectural

attributes of the home. This provides the fields of attributes I have identified with a deeper content and greater precision.

Each attribute field description concludes with an analysis of that field's symbolic importance for residents.

Materials and detailing

Residents are intimately concerned with materials and detailing, and when these aspects are well executed residents can perceive them as strong indications of care on their behalf.

The four case studies highlight two approaches to the specification of materials for the home. The first is exemplified by the apartments at Stumholmen and at Hestra. These projects are characterized by unusual and authentic materials that the residents can relate to in a strong and conscious way. The second approach is exemplified by the apartments at Lindholmen and Norrköping, which are characterized by a more traditional choice of materials of which residents have no outspoken opinion. The perception of materials in the home plays a more prominent role in residents' descriptions of their apartments in the Stumholmen and Hestra case studies than in the Lindholmen and Norrköping studies.

There is a genuineness and authenticity about many of the materials used in the Stumholmen apartments. The lime-washed pine floor is perceived as authentic because residents can understand its origins, its fabrication and its use. The authenticity of the wood floors makes it easy for residents to read them as signs of care for their well-being.

In the Hestra apartments, this authentic impression is strengthened by the sensitive siting of the buildings within the natural landscape. The site can be read as temporarily borrowed from nature. The wood floors in each room find symbolic resonance in the trees of the forest just outside the great glazed openings.

The loggia, Stumholmen.
Photo: Göran Peyronson.

Consideration for residents can also be perceived in the details. The glass block wall in the Lindholmen apartments, the sloped roofs at Hestra and the window detailing at Stumholmen are examples of how the form and expression of unusual details generate a feeling of consideration. An essential attribute of these signs of care is that they emerge as exceptions to what is considered standard and traditional. Unusual or personal materials and details are interpreted by residents as indications that they matter to someone.

The examination of materials and detailing in the four case studies indicates that the sense of consideration for residents can never be fixed or given an absolute value, but must always be seen in relation to the given site and situation.

The dining area at Lindholmen, the bay window at Norrköping, the opening between floors at Hestra and the loggia at Stumholmen are examples of inviting and welcoming features. Such details are profoundly im-

portant to the first impression of an apartment, a positive force that initiates the process of appropriation.

The good craftsmanship found at Stumholmen was not remarked upon by the residents there during my interviews with them. It is likely that deftly and properly executed workmanship is something that residents take for granted. On the other hand, residents did take note of the shortcomings at Lindholmen and Norrköping. Poor workmanship has a destructive effect that impedes the process of appropriation. No one wants to identify with poor workmanship.

The following spatial attributes and interdependent relationships are important to the perception of materials and detailing in the four case studies:

- Residents are intimately concerned with materials and detailing, and when these aspects are well executed they can perceive them as strong indications of thoughtfulness on their behalf.

- Materials that are perceived as genuine and authentic make it easy for residents to read them as signs of care for their well-being. This sense of authenticity depends on the ability of residents to understand a material's origins, fabrication and use.

- Care can in a very concrete way enhance the self-image of residents and be interpreted by them as confirmation of their value to society. Materials and detailing thereby offer the conditions for initiating the process by which residents appropriate their homes. Residents interpret the use of authentic materials and well-designed details as signs that they mean something to someone.

- The choice of materials and the detailing of the Stumholmen and Hestra apartments demonstrate that the sense of care depends on more than just exclusive design. Consideration can be equally well-expressed by the use of surprising or unusual design that questions the common and traditional.

- The sense of care for residents can never be fixed or given an absolute value, but must always be seen in relation to the given site and situation.

- Poor workmanship, sloppily designed details and materials that are perceived as inauthentic all have a destructive effect that impedes the process of appropriation.

Axiality

The four case studies demonstrate different architectural expressions of axiality in the home. At Hestra and Norrköping, directional axes combine with movement to clarify the organization of spaces. Step by step, the apartment is presented one part at a time. At Lindholmen and at Stumholmen, much of the architecture is revealed immediately from the entrance

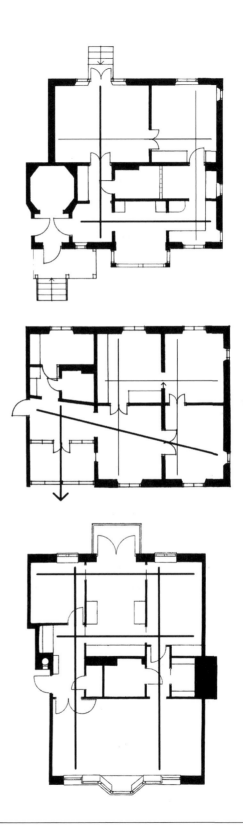

The apartment's axiality. Case studies 1, 2 and 4. Scale 1:200.

through views along a system of axes. Axiality helps clarify the organization of all of the apartments studied.

A comparison of the case studies can highlight several significant general attributes of axes.

The starting point of an axis is important in determining its dignity. Its goal creates anticipation that encourages movement along the axis. The flood of daylight that fills a group of windows, a balcony door or a bay window are examples from the case studies of axis goals that are also important architectural features in their own right. The dignity of an axis also depends upon the number of rooms it crosses. Thus the primary axes at Lindholmen and Stumholmen connect three rooms, while most of the secondary axes connect only two.

The main axes at Lindholmen and Stumholmen are quite long, spanning from one end of the apartment to the other. Most of the subsidiary axes are shorter and connect more limited areas. The dignity of an axis also depends on the appearance of the openings between rooms, the points of spatial connection along the axis. In the Lindholmen and Stumholmen apartments, the openings through which the primary axes pass are wide archways or French doors. There is a marked contrast to the treatment of the secondary axes, which connect rooms through standard-sized doors. Finally, the dignity of an axis is influenced by similarities, symmetries and activities in the rooms. For example, the main axis at Stumholmen integrates three rooms with similar materials and detailing, two of which are also the same size.

The following spatial attributes and interdependent relationships are important to the perception of axiality in the four case studies:

- The length of the axes is important to the effect of axiality. Long axes have more dignity than do short axes.
- The number of spaces connected by an axis is important. Axes that cross many rooms are perceived as dignified.
- Similarities, symmetries and repetition among the rooms connected by an axis lend dignity to the axis.
- The form of the openings between rooms is important. Broad openings contribute to the dignity of an axis.
- The starting point and goal of an axis influence the impression it makes. Axes that clearly connect important parts of a home are perceived as dignified.

Axiality is also influenced by symbolic values. It is tied to the visual impressions offered from the various axial starting points. These impressions generate expectations that can be physically confirmed by moving along the axis. The full effect of this field of attributes relies on this movement, giving movement an important impact on axiality. Thus the perception of axiality involves the establishment of a direct physical relationship to the architecture of the home.

Directional axes can visually articulate and emphasize important features of the home. Axiality is a part of and support for the process of appropriation by residents. Axes play an important role in the integration of interior and exterior space by leading to important points of contact between the two. This is the case in the hall at Stumholmen, where the primary longitudinal axis meets the powerful opening to the sea. The same happens in the Lindholmen dining area, where axes meet at the primary point of visual contact with the courtyard.

Enclosure

The case studies deal with rooms of varying degrees of spatial enclosure. The apartments at Stumholmen and Hestra have dramatically contrasting open and closed rooms. At Lindholmen and Norrköping the contrasts are more subtle. Three of the four projects – Stumholmen, Norrköping and Lindholmen – have rooms with clearly defined forms.

The legibility of spatial form is enhanced by strongly articulated corners where two walls meet and where the walls meet the ceiling. At Stumholmen the contours of the rooms are emphasized by the fact that the uppermost part of the walls is painted white, contrasting with the coloured wallpaper. This forms a connective framework that encloses the room, underlining its form.

The detailing of the openings in a room influences its relative open or closed character. The splayed niches at Stumholmen emphasize the thickness and mass of the walls. Accentuating the massiveness of a wall increases our impression of its protective and enclosing effect. At Stumholmen, the windows themselves have divided lights, a feature which articulates the boundary between interior and exterior space. The glazing bars suggest the plane of the wall before it was opened.

The thickness of the walls is not as clearly expressed at Lindholmen and Hestra. The walls have more the character of an envelope than a surrounding mass. Setting the windows flush with the surface of the walls gives no clear signal as to the character of the walls themselves.

The placement of openings is also of great impor-

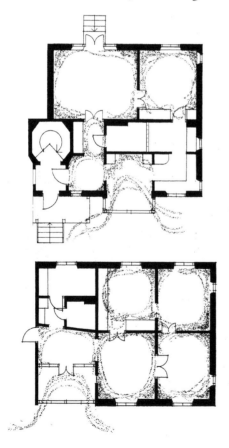

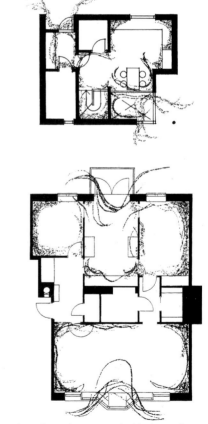

The apartment's enclosure, marked in heavy lines.
Case studies 1, 2, 3 and 4. Scale 1:200.

Hestra, bedroom, ground floor,
enclosed space.

tance. Stumholmen and Hestra are polar opposites in this respect. At Stumholmen the openings are generally placed symmetrically, with a section of wall above and below each window, and solid wall surfaces to either side. The openings are subordinate to the form of the walls. The placement of the windows gives the rooms strongly articulated corners, which enhances the legibility of the shape of the space. The same is true of the door openings at Stumholmen, where the header over each door clarifies the relationship between the enclosing wall and the opening in it. The door openings are fitted with thresholds that strengthen the contours of the room by articulating the original unbroken form of the wall. This diminishes the impact of the opening and increases the enclosure of the room.

Hestra. Open living room in two-bedroom apartment with large glazed openings and a wall screen where the strip window breaches the wall's meeting with the ceiling. Photo: Ulf Nilsson.

At Hestra, strip windows along the eaves of the upper level and windows that wrap around corners give a sense of spatial openness, a feeling augmented by the use of large glazed openings.

At Lindholmen there are no thresholds between kitchen, dining area and hall. The lack of spatial articulation along the edge of the floor, combined with a unity of flooring material in these three rooms, helps integrate the spaces.

In the case study apartments, the clarity and legibility of the spatial figures is a stronger determinant of the degree of enclosure than the plan and section of the rooms. The living room at Stumholmen is nearly square and clearly enclosed. The dining area at Lindholmen is also nearly square, but the large windows make the room open.

The following spatial attributes and interdependent relationships are important to the perception of enclosure in the four case studies:

- *The number of openings*: many openings increase the sense of openness.
- *The size of the openings*: large openings increase the sense of openness.
- *The placement of the openings in the walls*: symmetrical placement adds to the sense of enclosure.
- *The form of the openings*: details such as divided lights and thresholds convey an image of the uninterrupted form of the wall, making the space more legible, and therefore adding to the sense of enclosure.

The formal clarity and legibility of a room: this adds to the sense of enclosure.

- *Strongly articulated corners and unbroken wall surfaces*: these add to the sense of enclosure.
- *The form of the walls*: framing the openings with uninterrupted wall surfaces adds to the sense of enclosure.
- *Clearly defined spatial contours*: these add to the sense of enclosure.

- *Walls that give the impression of great mass*: these give a room a stronger sense of enclosure.

The enclosure of the rooms of a home is also important to the relationship between the building and its site, between the personal space of experience and the surrounding natural environment. The formation of an interior space can focus attention on important elements in the world outside, thereby supporting the process of appropriation. The relationship between openness and enclosure can prepare residents for discovering the conditions in their exterior surroundings.

One quality that the four case studies have in common is flexibility and ambiguity in the relationship between inside and out. Enclosing spaces are more common, but in each case such rooms are complemented by instances of nearly boundless openness and contact with the outdoors. The Hestra apartment's window walls, two metres (six feet) wide and two storeys high, almost dissolve the boundary to the outside, offering the exterior access to the private space of the interior.

Movement

The importance of movement to the architecture of the home depends upon its interaction with other fields of attributes. As we have seen, movement is extremely important to the impression of axiality. Movement along an axis gives us a direct physical relationship to the architecture of the home because only through movement can we explore and conquer its rooms.

Three of the case study apartments – Lindholmen, Stumholmen and Norrköping – offer residents the ability to walk a circular loop from room to room. At Hestra the movement is radial, with the hall and stairway providing access to the other spaces.

The circuit pattern allows each room to be experienced both in isolation and as part of an integrated whole. It causes the character of the individual rooms, for example in terms of daylight or enclosure, to work together. The ability to walk a complete loop through an apartment increases the wealth of experience it offers. The opportunity to enter a room from different directions is a resource and a necessary condition for the flexible use of the apartment. While some residents choose to close off this circuit, the freedom to do so must be seen as one of the qualities of this circulation pattern. The circuit increases the flexibility of all three apartments in which it appears.

The circuit pattern is most clearly expressed in Norrköping. It allows us to pass through rooms of varying illuminance, size and content, and takes us through all three parts of the home. The two longitudinal axes on the courtyard side add to the number of options, and the sequence of rooms along the facade encourages a sweeping movement through the apartment.

The rhythm of a movement depends upon the form and size of the rooms. Orientation within a larger space requires more time than is needed in more immediately legible smaller spaces. The ability to read a space influences the speed with which we move through it, providing a certain rhythm to our movement through a sequence of rooms. For example, the rhythm of the loop at Stumholmen is even, while the circulation patterns at Lindholmen and Norrköping are marked by greater variation. The great differences between the rooms along the transverse axes of the Norrköping apartment give drama and rhythm to the movement. Rhythm adds to our movements a physical relationship to the impression of the home. One way it can do this is through axiality, as previously described. Another way is by slowing the pace of our movement to allow us to register the information necessary to orient ourselves in larger spaces.

Daylight is a primary tool for orchestrating movement through the home, building on the physiological urge for humans to move from darker to brighter spaces. This occurs in various ways in the four case studies: the Stumholmen loggia and the Hestra floor opening are two extremely well-lit spaces that are contrasted by darker sequences of spaces; the bay windows in the Lindholmen dining area and the Norrköping

Movement through a chain of rooms, Stumholmen.
Photo: Göran Peyronson.

living room offer a visual goal for the movement from darkness to light, examples of how bright spaces inspire movement in each apartment. The loggia, floor opening and two bay windows in these examples are brightly lit rooms that act as border spaces in which contact can develop between the private space of the interior and the public space of the exterior. In each case study, movement helps focus attention on important features such as these.

The Norrköping apartment includes a movement that can be traced back to the way in which the middle-class home of the nineteenth century was used. It is a ritualized movement through a number of rooms with an air of formality. The functions of these rooms are easily recognizable elements in the traditional home: larger rooms for socializing and for dining, smaller rooms (such as the smoking room) for just a few of the guests. At Norrköping an old traditional organization of spaces has been reinterpreted for a new apartment.

The Lindholmen apartment exemplifies another kind of historically based movement. Here we have a sequence of outdoor spaces that become increasingly intimate and private as we approach the home.

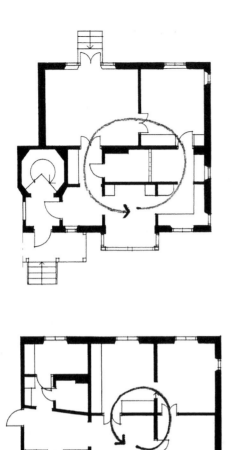

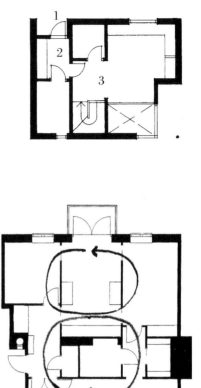

The apartment's movements. Case studies 1, 2, 3 and 4.
Scale 1:200.

The design of the courtyard and the boundaries that divide it stem from historical precedents.

The following spatial attributes and interdependent relationships are important to the perception of movement in the four case studies:

- The rhythm of a movement depends upon the form and size of the rooms. Orientation within a larger space requires more time than is needed in more immediately legible smaller spaces. Movement through a sequence of spaces therefore becomes rhythmic. The daylight, form and size of the rooms determine how dynamic the rhythm will be.

- The orchestrated movement through a sequence of spaces can utilize contrasts between darkness and light. In the four case studies this happens in two ways: first by adding an element of surprise, and second by using the brightest points as goals for directional axes that start in darker rooms.

- Some movement patterns carry associations to older traditional homes, adding temporal depth to the home.

Spatial figure

Spatial figure depends on a room's furnishings, openings, symmetry and size. Smaller rooms are often fitted with built-in cabinetry, which can obscure their shape in plan or section. Examples include the hanging rods and hat-rack in the walk-in cupboard at Stumholmen and the kitchen cabinetry at Lindholmen. The perception of spatial figure in medium-sized rooms can also be affected by furnishings, as in the case of the kitchens at Stumholmen and Norrköping, and even by the presence of large beds in the bedrooms. Large rooms generally have enough volume to allow spatial figure to be fully expressed.

The placement of a room's openings are vital to how we experience its spatial figure. The loggia in the Stumholmen apartments is 3.6 × 1.8m (11.8 × 5.9ft), a long, narrow spatial figure. The glazing on the longer sides creates an open space with a direction that is transverse to its narrow spatial figure. Despite similar proportions, a typical bedroom from a 1960s apartment, for example, is perceived in an entirely different way. The room in the illustration is only 2m (6.6ft) wide and 5m (16.4ft) long. The door and window openings are placed at opposite short ends. The room is perceived as very narrow, with long sides, which close in around the observer. The closeness of the side walls makes the openings at the ends all the more important. These openings enhance the impact of the room's long, narrow spatial figure and the longitudinal direction through it.

The symmetry and legibility of rooms also relate to our perception of spatial figure. This is illustrated by a comparison between the smaller bedroom at Norrköping and one of the Stumholmen living rooms. Both spaces are nearly square in plan and are similar in section. The Norrköping bedroom has three openings asymmetrically arranged on the side towards the kitchen – a swing door, a sliding door and a window. The location of each follows its own conditions. As a result, one side of the room seems open and one side closed, one

Bedroom in an apartment from the district of Hjällbo, Gothenburg, from 1967–69.

side light and one dark. The impression of the room's openings, its integration with adjoining spaces, its contact with the kitchen and its asymmetrical composition overshadow the impression of its square proportions. Spatial figure here plays a subordinate role: the proportions in plan and section have little effect on the perception of the space.

In contrast, in the Stumholmen living room the spatial figure is clearly perceived due to the combined effects of various details. The room's openings and wall surfaces are symmetrically composed and balanced. It is evenly illuminated with natural light and its contours are articulated. This room has clearly defined corners. There is no built-in cabinetry to disturb our perception of the plan form. The room has an unusual size and volume. Its 14m^2 (150 sq ft) area lies between the standard large bedroom and the standard living room. The ceiling height is 2.6m (8.5ft) instead of the normal 2.4m (8ft). The clarity of the space, together with its spaciousness, allows it to accommodate furniture without compromising its character. Our impression of this room's spatial figure is the product of all of these factors.

The living room in the Norrköping apartment has a width-to-length ratio of 1:2. The door openings and the large bay window are located on the long sides of the room. In this case it is the placement of the openings that determines our perception of the form of the room. The bay window emphasizes the centre of the room, thereby dividing up the space and countering the oblong plan form. The strength of the bay window causes the predominant direction to go through it rather than along the length of the room.

Spatial figure is also influenced by static and dynamic composition. Most of the dynamic spaces demonstrated are in the Hestra apartments. The living room and kitchen are quite open to the exterior as well as to the adjacent rooms. Their plan and sectional shapes are irregular. The dynamic impression they create is heightened by their position on the boundary between the private bedrooms and the public courtyard.

In the four case studies there are no clear or demonstrable connections between the proportions of the rooms, the impressions they make on residents and the intentions of the architects. My interviews turned up few comments by residents or architects regarding spatial proportions.

Throughout history the evaluation of rooms has often been based on various established systems of

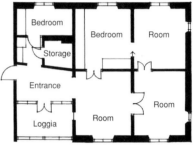

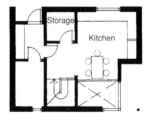

Floor plans. Case studies 1, 2, 3 and 4.
Scale 1:400.

proportion. These judgements are subjective and change over the course of history. None of the architects in the case studies consciously used proportional systems in the design of the buildings. Instead they worked more intuitively, as Hestra architect Jens Arnfred in particular pointed out.

It is important that we see these proportional systems as they were meant to be seen. Van der Laan compares his 'Plastic Number' with various musical scales. But using set relationships between tones does not guarantee a composer will produce good music. Musical composition relies on an understanding of scales and tonal relationships, but also on the creative manipulation of those scales and tones.

Proportional rules and systems must be seen as a possible starting point for an architect's design work, though it is his or her artistry in building on them that determines the result. Systems of proportion can provide inspiration and support in the planning process, but they can also seem restrictive. A rule book can never cover all of the complexity of a built space, building or public place.

The following spatial attributes and interdependent relationships are important to the perception of spatial figure in the four case studies:

- The size of a room is important to the impression of spatial figure. Spatial figure is likely to be perceived most clearly in rooms of large volume.
- The symmetrical arrangement of openings and furnishings helps clarify spatial figure.
- The perception of a room's proportions is influenced by its size, furnishing, openings, daylight conditions and movement, and its relationship to adjacent spaces.

Among the apartments surveyed, room proportions can most easily be registered at Stumholmen. In the other apartments, our perception of spatial figure is dominated by other attributes, such as openness, views and integration with the exterior.

Benedictine monastery outside Tomelilla, designed strictly in compliance with the 'Plastic Number'.

Daylight

A readily observable indication of the importance of daylight is how it influences the other fields of attributes. Daylight plays an important role in defining the starting points and goals of axes at Lindholmen, Stumholmen and Norrköping, and in inspiring movement along those axes. Contrasts in illuminance make movement along an axis more eventful. At Lindholmen and Norrköping, variations in lighting conditions give axial movements a certain rhythm. At Hestra and Stumholmen, the daylight that floods spaces in the border region between inside and out helps make these spaces compelling goals in sequences of events that have been orchestrated by the architects. Daylight conditions also help define the degree of enclosure in a room: subdued lighting gives a room a more enclosed character, while bright light contributes to a sense of openness.

In each case study, daylight plays a significant role in establishing a relationship between interior and exterior space. Daylight helps accentuate important places in the home. Examples of this include the dining area at

Intense light. A combination of direct and reflected light.
Window in Äshults by, Halland.

there is a sufficient amount of both direct and reflected light. At Stumholmen, reflections from the sea generate a tremendous amount of daylight. Glazing bars and moulded details in the windows, along with the extra wide splayed side surfaces of the window embrasures, offer plenty of surfaces for reflecting the incoming sunlight. At Hestra, the expanse of the window openings is responsible for the wealth of daylight. In addition, the broad white surfaces that surround the space generate large amounts of reflected light.

The light that results in these places has a condensed character. Both rooms have small and concentrated forms that frame the mix of direct and reflected light. The condensed light thus produced articulates the breach in the facade and the interface with the space outside.

The light that fills the openings in the outside walls emphasizes their enclosing function. These walls are to divide the thoroughly sunlit natural environment from the more selectively illuminated space of the interior. A glazed opening creates a visual connection between interior and exterior space, while it also forms a distinct boundary for the particular qualities of each. The walls of the home separate the two, and the rays of the sun admitted to the interior by openings in these walls symbolize what the interior and exterior have in common. At the same time the incoming daylight articulates the differences between inside and out, serving as a reminder of the presence of the natural world just outside the home.

The bright light outside the more dimly lit private interior of the home also helps initiate the process of appropriation. The spatial movement from darkness to light continues into the space outside. Daylight thus underlines the possibility of movement between inside and out.

The relationship of a room and its walls to the openings in those walls is visually clarified by the play of light across the details of the opening. The design of the home for daylight, particularly in the openings to the outside, thus becomes an important element in the

Lindholmen, the space in the opening between floors at Hestra, the bay window at Norrköping and the loggia at Stumholmen. These rooms serve as the high points in a sequence of increasing illuminance. Daylight conveys meaning by describing and giving character to the relationship between a home and its surroundings. The effectiveness of daylighting strategies depends on the presence of darkness as a background.

There is an unusual intensity in the light that fills the window niches at Stumholmen and the floor opening at Hestra. This intensity is the product of the combination between direct and reflected light. It arises when the two are concentrated on the same spot, and when process of appropriation by residents – one component in their identification with the place and their creation of meaning – since it makes the courtyard or grounds around the building into an integral part of the home. The light-filled opening provides concrete evidence for this relationship, as exemplified by the intense light in the Stumholmen window niches or the glass walls at Hestra.

What I have described as the concentration of light articulates the path between the interior and exterior spaces. This concentrated light is an important part of the creation of meaning in residents' appropriation of their homes.

The following spatial attributes and interdependent relationships are important to the perception of daylight in the four case studies:

- *Concentrated light.* In focused, bounded spaces that are flooded with both direct and indirect daylight we find the conditions for concentrated light. This concentrated light shows the importance of the openings in the outside wall in establishing the relationship between the home and the surrounding exterior environment.
- *Symbolically laden light.* Daylight illuminates the differences between the private space of the interior of the home and the public space outside, and also emphasizes the important features and events of the home. The rays of sunlight that penetrate through the openings symbolize what the interior and exterior have in common. Creating sequences of spaces with varying daylight conditions can help articulate the interface between inside and out.
- *Daylight has a decisive influence on all of the other fields of attributes.* It provides goals for axes and movements and helps strengthen the character of enclosure in a room.

At Hestra, the high and wide window openings give a lot of light. Large, light surfaces enclose the room and provide it with plenty of reflected light. Photo: Ulf Nilsson.

Organization of spaces

The four case studies are the products of different trends in architectural history, and these differences are reflected in their layouts. The Hestra apartments carry traces of the Functionalist home. The Stumholmen apartments have certain similarities to Classical precedents, and at Lindholmen and Norrköping we find elements of both Functionalism and Classicism.

One thing all four have in common is that in various ways they all demonstrate possible areas of development for the standard Functionalist apartment. Examples include the carefully balanced and sensitive siting of the Hestra apartments, the generalized rooms and Classicist plan at Stumholmen, and the circular circulation pattern and longitudinal divisions of the apartments at Lindholmen and Norrköping.

Each of the apartments studied has an unusual historical connection due either to its treatment of the site or the temporal depth of its spatial organization. The Lindholmen apartments are an example of how the simple pre-Functionalist apartment's precise delineation of territory and boundaries can be recreated. The

General rooms in a flexible plan.
Stumholmen. Scale 1:200.

Hestra apartments build on an approach to site-planning that developed progressively until the end of the 1950s. At Hestra, many of the ideals that could not be realized earlier have come to fruition, such as the small scale of the development and the flexibility in the meeting between the buildings and the site. The Norrköping building is well suited to the neighbouring buildings, yet is architecturally distinguished and a reflection of its own time.

Residential architecture during the Functionalist era was divided into specific building types: the slab, the tower, terraced housing and the balcony-access block. Among the four case studies, Stumholmen and Norrköping can be considered slabs with stairwells that serve two units per floor. The Stumholmen building is a narrow slab, hardly 8m (26ft) deep, while the building in Norrköping is a 12m (40ft) thick slab.

The Lindholmen project cannot be accurately described by any of the Functionalist archetypes. An appropriate designation would perhaps be to call it a 'little apartment building' or a 'house in the city', since it has only a few apartments grouped around a single stairwell. This form of construction was common in Sweden during the 1940s and 1950s, particularly in small towns. Hestra appears to be based on the concept of terraced housing developed into a multi-family apartment building. The terraced houses' private garden plots have been incorporated into the public domain, which provides the conditions for a uniquely sensitive treatment of the site. The architect has been able to preserve the largely untouched natural landscape that surrounds his buildings. He has created a new kind of multi-family apartment building with similarities to the 'little apartment building' and the 'house in the city' but with the reverential and volatile relationship of the hunting lodge to its natural setting.

An important attribute of the Stumholmen apartment is the breadth of interpretation it can sustain. The architect has established a framework for these interpretations and set the limits of the possibilities. The depth of interpretation is built up of attributes that work at various levels. The interaction between materials, detailing and form results in rooms with a great deal of dignity, but does not limit them to specific functions. Instead the rooms are designed to be general and their content and meaning are not determined until someone inhabits them. The organization of spaces at Stumholmen aligns walk-through rooms in rows, a rejection of the Functionalist apartment's radial circulation pattern of dead-end rooms surrounding a neutral point of access. Stumholmen's three-part layout makes possible a variety of activities, characters and degrees of privacy. The generality of the rooms and the flexibility of their arrangement provide the conditions necessary for residents to interpret their living conditions individually. The depth of interpretation thus afforded is essential to the creation of meaning in the home.

A home is made up of a series of rooms that lie between the public space of the natural environment and the personal space of experience within each of us. In the case studies we can see two types of meeting between building and site that have implications for the relationship between public and private. At Lindholmen and Hestra, the home meets the outside world through a sequence of different spatial and territorial formations. The design of the interior spaces prepares us for the meeting with the exterior. At Norrköping and Stumholmen, interior and exterior meet more directly, without intervening border spaces.

The various territorial demarcations found around the Lindholmen apartments help the residents establish personal territory. Symbols taken from the historic building environment that surrounds the project – boundaries between home, courtyard and street space – have been reinterpreted to provide residents with important support in appropriating their surroundings. The dining area contributes to this appropriation by allowing the residents to inhabit the boundary between inside and outside. The clearly delineated boundaries that divide the courtyard into regions of varying privacy make it possible for the residents to adopt the common space around the home one section at a time. The dining area is set into a bay window, making it the most open place in the apartment and expressing its function as a border space, setting up a visual meeting between the residents inside and their neighbours outside. The openness of the dining area allows residents to appraise the appearance and affiliation of the various territorial regions.

The boundaries at Hestra work in a similar fashion. The buildings' simplicity and sensitive siting provide conditions for residents to establish territory. The open space between floors allows them to inhabit the border region between inside and out – limiting the steadily increasing openness of the interior spaces, and at the same time limiting the growing level of privacy and enclosure of the exterior space as it approaches the home. Borders inside and out allow the residents to appropriate the home in phases, and the openness of the scheme allows them to orient themselves visually in the territory outside as well as estimate to whom it belongs.

At Hestra and Lindholmen, residents have established clearly defined territories outside of their homes. Parts of the space outside are used as an extension of the home. Alternatively, the Norrköping apartments are designed for a more traditional urban lifestyle in which residents do not use the site or the courtyard as an

Norrköping. Facade facing the street Nya Rådustugugatan.

extension of the home. The boundaries of each apartment also mark the limits of the inhabitants' territory. The balcony over the courtyard and the bay window towards the street are two points at which those boundaries are called into question.

During the summer, residents at Stumholmen can make use of the area next to the building, but must share that space with visitors and with the island's other inhabitants. While the island itself serves as something of a territorial region, the next, though smaller, clearly demarcated border is the apartment building. This building demonstrates a problematic relationship between the home and its surroundings. The lack of delineated zones of progressively increasing privacy allows strangers to come too close to the private space of the home. Though the building stands in a park, it has the same kind of relationship to its surroundings as the urban building at Norrköping, and as a result its territorial relationships are unclear.

The presence of border spaces is an important part of residents' perception of identity in the home. Border spaces serve to mediate between a building and its surroundings, since they seem to belong to both public and private spheres. They are part of the home, and at the same time part of the public space beyond the home's protective walls.

The Norrköping and Lindholmen apartments have border spaces in the form of bay windows. Stumholmen has its loggia and Hestra its space in the opening between floors, the broad glazing of each giving it a spatial openness. Various fields of attributes combine in these border spaces.

At Hestra and Stumholmen, in addition to helping residents establish territory, border spaces bring in nature, making it a tangible part of the life of the home. This is where residents are directly confronted with the natural environment. The border space at Hestra is an important room for the residents – their comments attest to the fact that it is loaded with symbolic value.

The daylight in such a border space is deeply appreciated by the residents. It is no exaggeration to claim that natural light is extremely important for many of us: many assert that melancholy is a direct consequence of dark winters, and we therefore have a psychological need for daylight. The border spaces we have studied are devoted to the ritualized meeting with daylight that is such a fundamental aspect of our culture.

The woods surrounding the Hestra apartments remind their inhabitants that someone cared enough about their well-being to have conscientiously preserved the natural environment during construction. They feel like nature is present even inside their apartments.

Border spaces also address our need for control over our territory. They allow us to move between inside and outside, and across territorial boundaries. A border

Border space, Hestra. Glazed section, two floors high, in front of the room with the floor opening.

space is a point from which to survey and therefore guard our territory.

We also have a psychological need to socialize, to interact with others, and this requires appropriate public places. Many claim that the public realm is in decline and that there is a shortage of space in which such social interaction can take place. Border spaces address our need to meet others. From these open rooms we can see and be seen, participating visually in the public realm, yet sheltered by the safety of our own private space. They are both public and private, and can serve as substitutes for lost public space.

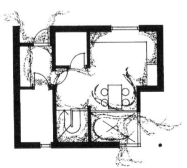

Border space, Hestra, marked in heavy lines on a four-bedroom apartment's entry level. Scale 1:400.

At Hestra, the relationships between interior space, border space and exterior space have been carefully thought out and thoroughly designed. The architecture of the border space is extremely important to our experience there: it is a room with strong identity, one in which the residents truly enjoy spending time.

The border spaces at Hestra, Stumholmen and Norrköping are rooms that are not dedicated to specific activities. They therefore lie outside of the framework of strict functional categorization that characterizes the Functionalist home. Here residents are free to merely observe their surroundings without purpose or obligation.

The satisfaction residents clearly expressed in all four case studies indicates a successful appropriation of the home. My analyses have shown that the architecture of the home is an important factor in creating identity, of great importance to residents in establishing territory.

The design of the home and its surroundings can provide an important support to the process of appropriation. This is most obvious at Lindholmen and Hestra, where dividing the exterior space into zones of varying degree of privacy allows residents to appropriate their environment gradually. One area at a time can be added to the private, secure territory. In sharing the responsibility for maintaining the courtyard at Lindholmen, residents demonstrate their control over their territorial rights. They plant and cultivate the area to mark their territory. At both Lindholmen and Hestra, historical remnants and patterns offer support in the appropriation process. The broadly glazed openings of their border spaces express their affiliation with and control over part of the surrounding territory.

At Hestra, the forested site is of great symbolic importance. The conservation of the natural environment during construction is interpreted by residents as a sign of care and thus helps initiate the process of appropriation. The presence of historical traces such as old gravel roads, stone fences and preserved old houses strengthens and develops that process. The grounds around the buildings at Hestra are also clearly divided

The courtyard.
Lindholmen.

by boundaries into territorial regions – outdoor room, courtyard, building cluster – that allow appropriation to be completed gradually, one area at a time.

The following spatial attributes and interdependent relationships are important to the perception of the organization of spaces in the four case studies:

• Each case study includes a border space – a room that is within the home but provides residents with an intimate connection to the exterior. At Hestra and Lindholmen these border spaces are part of a sequence of rooms that proceeds from inside to out.

This strengthens their roles as mediators between the two, making the border spaces important to the process by which residents appropriate their homes.

- Appropriation can be facilitated by the design of the home and its surroundings. At Lindholmen and Hestra the grounds around the building are clearly subdivided. The form of each piece of territory is underlined by traces of history. The presence of clear boundaries in the exterior space is an essential condition to the establishment of territory by residents.

- Appropriation is the process by which the interior of a residence is transformed into all that we associate with the word 'home'. If the inside space seems safe enough, parts of the outside may be incorporated into the home. In our culture, the perception of proximity to nature is important to this process. Proximity to nature may be conveyed visually, as at Stumholmen, or visually, physically and symbolically, as at Hestra.

Chapter 6

Conclusion

The outcome of my work is the identification of seven fields of attributes that are important to the architecture of the home. I have called these fields 'Materials and detailing', 'Axiality', 'Enclosure', 'Movement', 'Spatial figure', 'Daylight' and 'Organization of spaces'. I have defined a field of attributes as a distinguishable complex of details, attributes and characteristics. Each field is described in each of the case studies. Building on prior research and theoretical developments, I have outlined the concepts and conditions that are important to each field of attributes.

In the four case studies I have demonstrated how non-measurable architectural qualities appear in the home. In a comparative description I have discussed the spatial variables and relationships that influence our perception of non-measurable architectural attributes in the case study projects. By comparing these projects I have also been able to demonstrate the symbolic importance of some of these attributes to residents' impressions of their homes.

My central conclusions are: first, that these non-measurable attributes are indispensable to the quality of the home, and second that they are important to residents' perception of their homes and intimately connected to the process of appropriation and the creation of meaning.

A sense of reality

My analyses show that, taken together, the key elements of these fields of attributes can help create a sense of reality, contact with the present moment, which means they have a deep symbolic significance for residents. The experience is similar to that described by Magnus William-Olsson in his discussion of the ability of poetry to move us.[1] William-Olsson maintains that there is a connection between the activity of reading aloud and the powerful experience when the body – intuitively and subconsciously – is moved by our speech. The physical activity is important here: the total art experience requires the involvement of the body.

The architectural researcher Bobo Hjort has studied the importance of the connection between form and perception. He asserts that the brain uses two systems – one old and one new. The old biological system includes the subconscious, and controls feelings such as pleasure, desire, hunger and fear – feelings we cannot logically master or control. The new system, logical and learned, includes intelligence and our ability to analyse and expand our knowledge. Language is a central part of the new system, as is our ability to reflect. The two systems work together.[2]

In several of my interviews, residents described their relation to their homes in such strong terms as love. For example:

But when we came into the apartment, with the loggia, I for one fell madly in love with the place.

That was a Sunday, and on Monday we applied for that apartment right over there, but there was already a couple signed up, the people who live there now. We got this one instead. And that's how it happened.

(Personal interview (Britta), Britta and Bertil, two-bedroom apartment residents, Stumholmen)

An example of the ability of residential architecture to express a strong sense of presence and an awareness of the moment can be found in the directional axis. The perception of axiality in a home begins when we find ourselves at the starting point of an axis. The visual impression of an axis creates an anticipation that we can physically fulfil through movement. As it incorporates movement, axiality establishes a direct physical aspect to our perception of the architecture of the home, going one step beyond the purely visual perception.

Movement unites axiality with a sense of time, in part through the relationship of our expectations to future events, and in part as an awareness of the present moment, in the instant we fulfil and confirm our expectations. Visual and physical impressions are stored and become parts of the collected experience, memories that we will always carry with us. The relationship between axiality and time is important to our subconscious perception of the architecture of the home.

In a similar fashion, movement through the home is connected with our perception of time, proximity and reality. Like axiality, movement has a physical relationship to the architecture of the home. As has been described earlier, our movement slows subconsciously to allow us to register the information necessary to orient ourselves in a large space. This gives us a physical relationship to the size, shape and daylight conditions in each room, and to time. The rhythm of our movement is important to the subconscious perception of the home.

Another important subconscious aspect in our impression of architecture is the element of surprise that comes with movement through the home. The powerful contrast between Stumholmen's dark, enclosed stairwell and its brightly lit, open loggia gives a strong impression similar to the confirmation and fulfilment that is part of the sense of reality.

The physical, corporeal aspects of axiality and movement give them a relationship to the subconscious. In the attribute field I have called 'Daylight' there is a visual relationship to the sense of reality. The walls that surround the home separate the fully sunlit space of nature from the selectively lit space inside. The play of daylight in openings clarifies the enclosing function of the walls, but also contributes to our awareness of time. When the rays of the sun are refracted and reflected in the space of a window niche, a concentrated light is produced. This concentrated light makes manifest the path of light as it crosses from exterior to interior. Light is captured in the opening, its path delayed, thus connecting to the perception of time. The opening in a wall is therefore not merely a breach in the barrier between limited and limitless space, or between different lighting conditions; concentrated light turns a wall opening into a window on the present moment. The relationship between daylight and time is an important aspect of our subconscious impression of the architecture of the home.

The above description indicates that axiality, movement and daylight can help create a strong sense of reality and connect us with the present moment. In this respect, the perception of architecture is similar to the perception of other arts, such as poetry, sculpture, film and painting.

Residential architecture has an all-too-often overlooked potential to move us and influence our behaviour, as well as to enrich the daily life of its residents. This potential can be exploited without compromising the practical and functional aspects of the home. The architecture of the home can also encompass a wealth of varied impressions and a depth of interpretation through form, light and movement. Architecture can thereby offer support in the process by which residents appropriate their homes, while it can also move us and

elicit fundamental subconscious feelings such as desire and curiosity. One quotation from a resident interview deserves to be repeated here:

Interviewer: It sounds like some form of love at first sight.
Karin: Yes, it was – I thought the apartment was . . . I don't know, it was everything about the place. Part of it was that it wasn't the traditional, rectangular kind of construction, partly that there was so much light, and then that it had natural materials everywhere. Our last place had plastic trim and vinyl flooring. And then just the architecture. The light and the location – you look right out into nature.

(Personal interview, Karin, four-bedroom apartment resident, Hestra)

The four case studies demonstrate how all of these fields of attributes can be captured in the home. They show the wealth of meaning and existential depth that architecture can generate and cultivate in the heart of a resident. They illustrate how important the architecture of a home is to its inhabitants.

It is my hope that the observations gathered in this explorative study might help others to see housing design as a matter of architecture in the broadest possible sense.

Landscape with houses, water-colour,
Armand Björkman.

Notes

Chapter 1 **Introduction**
1. Daun, Åke (1980) *Boende och livsform* (Dwelling and Lifestyle, in Swedish only), in collaboration with Siv Ehn, Stockholm: Tiden in co-operation with insurance company Folksam's social committee, p. 72.
2. Andersson, Birgitta (1976) *Idealbostad eller nödbostad* (Ideal home or emergency housing), diss., Chalmers University of Technology, Sweden.
3. Ellen, Key (1899) *Hemmets århundrade* (The Century of the Home), Stockholm: Verdandi småskrifter.
4. Norberg-Schulz, Christian (1978) *Mellom jord og himmel* (Between Heaven and Earth, in Norwegian only), Oslo: Universitetsforlaget, p. 101.
5. Cornell, Elias (1968) *Arkitekturhistoria* (Architectural History, in Swedish only), Stockholm: Almqvist & Wiksell, p. 12.
6. Bachelard, Gaston (1964) *The Poetics of Space*, from 1994 edn, Boston: Beacon Press, p. 202.
7. Rybczynski, Witold (1988) *Home – a Short History of an Idea*, London: Heinemann, p. 95.

Chapter 2 **Conducting architectural research**
1. Glaser, Barney and Strauss, Anselm (1967) *The Discovery of Grounded Theory Method*, New York: Aldine.
2. Norberg-Schulz, Christian (1978) *Mellom jord og himmel* (Between Heaven and Earth, in Norwegian only), Oslo: Universitetsforlaget.
3. Bachelard, Gaston (1964) *The Poetics of Space*, from 1994 edn, Boston: Beacon Press.

4. Van der Laan, Dom Hans (1983) *Architectonic Space*, Leiden: Brill Academic Publishers.
5. William-Olsson, Magnus (1997) *Obegränsningens ljus* (The Boundlessness of Light, in Swedish only), Stockholm: Gedins Förlag.

Chapter 3 **Identifying fields of attributes**
1. Lefebvre, Henri (1991) *The Production of Space*, Oxford: Basil Blackwell.
2. Hurtig, Eva (1995) *Hemhörighet och stadsförnyelse* (A sense of belonging and urban renewal, in Swedish only), diss., Chalmers University of Technology, Sweden, p. 87.
3. Gromark, Sten (1993) *Befriande arkitektur: studier av nutida arkitektur I social förvandling* (Liberating architecture: Studies of contemporary architecture in social change, in Swedish only), Gothenburg: Department of Architecture, Chalmers University of Technology, p. 70.
4. Hjort, Bobo (1983) *Var hör människan hemma?* (Where do people belong? in Swedish only), 2nd edn, Stockholm: Division of Theoretical and Applied Aesthetics, Department of Architecture, Stockholm Technical Institute. First edition published as a doctoral dissertation with a summary in English, Division of Theoretical and Applied Aesthetics, Stockholm Technical Institute.
5. Andersson, Torbjörn (1993) 'Människan och miljön' (People and the environment, in Swedish only), *Miljonprogrammet* (The Million Programme, a common designation for the building boom of the 1960s), ed. Mats Theselius, Stockholm: Mama (Magasin för modern arkitektur – Magazine for Modern Architecture), p. 53.
6. Hesselgren, Sven (1969) *The Language of Architecture*, Lund: Studentlitteratur, p. 281.
7. Wallinder, Jan (1988) *Bild och bostad* (Visuality and the home, in Swedish only), *Arkitektur* 10.
8. Norberg-Schulz, Christian (1980) *Meaning in Western Architecture*, revised edn, London: Cassell, p. 131ff.
9. Bachelard, Gaston (1964) *The Poetics of Space*, from 1994 edn, Boston: Beacon Press.
10. Pallasmaa, Juhani (1996) 'Identity, intimacy and domicile', *The Home*, Hampshire: Averbury Publishing.
11. Andersson, Torbjörn (1993) 'Människan och miljön' (People and the environment, in Swedish only), *Miljonprogrammet* (The Million Programme, a common designation for the building boom of the 1960s), ed. Mats Theselius, Stockholm: Mama (Magasin för modern arkitektur – Magazine for Modern Architecture), p. 53.
12. Zevi, Bruno (1978) *The Language of Architecture*, Seattle: Washington University Press, p. 31.
13. Brochmann, Odd (1960) *Inne* (In, in Norwegian only), Oslo: J. W. Cappelens Förlag.

14. Wulz, Fredrik F. (1991) *Fasaden & stadsrummet* (The Facade and Urban Space, in Swedish only), Stockholm: Byggforlaget, p. 85 ff.

15. Bachelard, Gaston (1964) *The Poetics of Space,* from 1994 edn, Boston: Beacon Press.

16. Hillier, Bill and Hansson, Julienne (1984) *The Social Logic of Space,* Cambridge: Cambridge University Press, p. 146.

17. Norberg-Schulz, Christian (1978) *Mellom jord og himmel* (Between Heaven and Earth, in Norwegian only), Oslo: Universitetsforlaget, pp. 87–8.

18. Wulz, Fredrik F (1991) *Fasaden & stadsrummet* (The Facade and Urban Space, in Swedish only), Stockholm: Byggforlaget, p. 96.

19. Bergström, Inger (1996) *Rummet och människans rörelser* (Space and human movement, in Swedish only), diss., Chalmers University of Technology, Sweden, p. 81.

20. Hesselgren, Sven (1969) *The Language of Architecture,* Lund: Studentlitteratur, p. 331.

21. Strengell, Gustav (1922) *Stadens som konstverk* (The City as a Work of Art, in Swedish only), Stockholm: Bonnier, p. 47.

22. Hillier, Bill and Hansson, Julienne (1984) *The Social Logic of Space,* Cambridge: Cambridge University Press.

23. Le Corbusier (1948) 'L'architecture et l'esprit mathématique'. Translation can be found in Johan Linton's degree paper written for the School of Architecture, Chalmers University of Technology, Sweden, in 1996. Original article can be found in the Fondation Le Corbusier archives, Paris.

24. Le Corbusier (1958/1936) *The Home of Man,* London: The Architectural Press, p. 122.

25. Van der Laan, Hans Dom (1983) *Architectonic Space,* Leiden: Brill Academic Publishers.

26. William-Olsson, Magnus (1997) *Obegränsningens ljus* (The Boundlessness of Light, in Swedish only), Stockholm: Gedins Förlag.

27. Rasmussen, Sten Eiler (1959) *Experiencing Architecture,* London: Chapman & Hall, p. 186.

28. Ibid, p. 191.

29. *The Oxford Dictionary of English Etymology* (1966), Oxford: Oxford University Press.

30. Riley, Terence (1996) *Light Construction,* New York: Museum of Modern Art.

31. From interview with Kjell Forshed, 'Case study Stumholmen'.

32. Hesselgren, Sven (1969) *The Language of Architecture,* Lund: Studentlitteratur, p. 231.

33. Liljefors, Anders (1986) 'Att behärska ljuset' (Mastering Light, in Swedish only), *Arkitektur* 1.

34. *The Oxford Dictionary of English Etymology* (1966) Oxford: Oxford University Press.

35. Malmberg, Torsten (1983) *Räkna med revir* (Count on Territory, in Swedish only) Stockholm: Liber Förlag.

36. Hurtig, Eva (1995) 'Hemhörighet och stadsförnyelse' (A sense of belonging and urban renewal, in Swedish only), diss., Chalmers University of Technology, Sweden, p. 87.

37. Gromark, Sten (1993) *Befriande arkitektur: studier av nutida arkitektur I social förvandling* (Liberating Architecture: Studies of contemporary architecture in social change, in Swedish only), Gothenburg: Department of Architecture, Chalmers University of Technology, p. 70.

38. Wiklund, Tage (1995) *Det tillgjorda landskapet* (The Artificial Landscape, in Swedish only), Gotherburg: Korpen, p. 134.

39. Norberg-Schulz, Christian (1978) *Mellom jord og himmel* (Between Heaven and Earth, in Norwegian only), Oslo: Universitetsforlaget, p. 87.

40. Ibid.

41. Ibid.

Chapter 4 **Case studies**

1. Van der Laan, Dom Hans (1983) *Architectonic Space,* Leiden: Brill Academic Publishers.

2. Arnfred, Jens (1992) 'Hestra Parkstad' (Hestra Parktown, in Swedish only), *Arkitektur* 6.

3. Lindroos, Bengt (1989) And so on . . . , Stockholm: International Förlag, p. 51.

4. Ibid.

5. Ibid., p. 8.

Chapter 6 **Conclusion**

1. William-Olsson, Magnus (1997) *Obegränsningens ljus* (The Boundlessness of Light, in Swedish only), Stockholm: Gedins Förlag, p. 77.

2. Hjort, Bobo (1983) *Var hör människan hemma?* (Where do people belong? in Swedish only), 2nd edn, Stockholm: Division of Theoretical and Applied Aesthetics, Department of Architecture, Stockholm Technical Institute, p. 70ff. First edition published as a doctoral dissertation with a summary in English, Division of Theoretical and Applied Aesthetics, Stockholm Technical Institute.

Bibliography

Andersson, Birgitta (1976) 'Idealbostad eller nödbostad' (Ideal home or emergency housing, in Swedish only), diss., Chalmers University of Technology, Sweden.

Andersson, Torbjörn (1993) 'Människan och miljön' (People and the environment, in Swedish only), *Miljonprogrammet* (The Million Programme, a common designation for the building boom of the 1960s), ed. Mats Theselius, Stockholm: Mama (Magasin för modern arkitektur – Magazine for Modern Architecture).

Arnfred, Jens (1992) 'Hestra Parkstad', *Arkitektur* 6.

Bachelard, Gaston (1964) *The Poetics of Space,* from 1994 edn, Boston: Beacon Press.

Bergström, Inger (1996) 'Rummet och människans rörelser' (Space and human movement, in Swedish only), diss., Chalmers Univesity of Technology, Sweden.

Björkman, Armand (1988) *Skisser och sånt* (Sketches and Similar Things), Stockholm: Arkitektur.

Brochmann, Odd (1960) *Inne* (In, in Norwegian only), Oslo: J. W. Cappelens Forlag.

Cornell, Elias (1968) *Arkitekturhistoria* (Architectural History, in Swedish only), Stockholm: Almqvist & Wiksell.

Daun, Åke (1980) *Boende och livsform* (Dwelling and Lifestyle, in Swedish only), in collaboration with Siv Ehn, Stockholm: Tiden in co-operation with insurance company Folksam's social committee.

Glaser, Barney and Strauss, Anselm (1967) *The Discovery of Grounded Theory Method,* New York: Aldine.

Gromark, Sten (1993) *Befriande arkitektur: studier av nutida arkitektur I social förvandling* (Liberating Architecture: Studies of contemporary architecture in social change, in Swedish only), Gothenburg: Department of Architecture, Chalmers University of Technology.

Hesselgren, Sven (1969) *The Language of Architecture*, Lund: Studentlitteratur.

Hillier, Bill and Hansson, Julienne (1984) *The Social Logic of Space*, Cambridge: Cambridge University Press.

Hjort, Bobo (1983) *Var hör människan hemma?* (Where do people belong? in Swedish only), 2nd edn, Stockholm: Division of Theoretical and Applied Aesthetics, Department of Architecture, Stockholm Technical Institute. First edition published as a doctoral dissertation with a summary in English, Division of Theoretical and Applied Aesthetics, Stockholm Technical Institute.

Hurtig, Eva (1995) 'Hemhörighet och stadsförnyelse' (A sense of belonging and urban renewal, in Swedish only), diss., Chalmers University of Technology, Sweden.

Key, Ellen (1899) *Hemmets århundrade* (The Century of the Home, in Swedish only), Stockholm: Verdandi småskrifter.

Le Corbusier (1948) 'L'architecture et l'esprit mathématique'. Translation can be found in Johan Linton's degree paper written for the School of Architecture, Chalmers University of Technology, Sweden, in 1996. Original article can be found in the Fondation Le Corbusier archives, Paris.

Le Corbusier (1958/1936) *The Home of Man*, London: The Architectural Press.

Lefebvre, Henri (1991) *The Production of Space*, Oxford: Basil Blackwell.

Liljefors, Anders (1986) 'Att behärska ljuset' (Mastering light, in Swedish only), *Arkitektur* 1.

Lindroos, Bengt (1989) And so on . . . , Stockholm: International Förlag.

Norberg-Schulz, Christian (1978) *Mellom jord og himmel* (Between Heaven and Earth, in Norwegian only) Oslo: Universitetsforlaget.

Norberg-Schulz, Christian (1980) *Meaning in Western Architecture,* revised edn, London: Cassell.

The Oxford Dictionary of English Etymology, (1966) Oxford: Oxford University Press.

Pallasmaa, Juhani (1996) 'Identity, intimacy and domicile', *The Home,* Hampshire: Avebury Publishing.

Rasmussen, Sten, Eiler (1959) *Experiencing Architecture,* London: Chapman & Hall.

Riley, Terence (1996) *Light Construction,* New York: Museum of Modern Art.

Rybczynski, Witold (1988) *Home – a Short History of an Idea,* London: Heinemann, p. 95.

Strengell, Gustav (1922) *Stadens som konstverk* (The City as a Work of Art, in Swedish only), Stockholm: Bonnier.

Van der Laan, Hans Dom (1983) *Architectonic Space*, Leiden: Brill Academic Publishers.

Wallinder, Jan (1988) 'Bild och bostad' (Visuality and the home, in Swedish only), *Arkitektur* 10.

Wiklund, Tage (1995) *Det tillgjorda landskapet* (The Artificial Landscape, in Swedish only), Gothenburg: Korpen.

William-Olsson, Magnus (1997) *Obegränsningens ljus* (The Boundlessness of Light, in Swedish only), Stockholm: Gedins Förlag.

Witold, Rybczynski (1988/1986) *Home – a Short History of an Idea*, London: Heinemann.

Wulz, Fredrik F (1991) *Fasaden & stadsrummet*, (The Facade and Urban Space, in Swedish only), Stockholm: Byggforlaget.

Zevi, Bruno (1978) *The Modern Language of Architecture*, Seattle: Washington University Press.